# The Damned Don't Drown

# The Damned Don't Drown

The *Wilhelm Gustloff* was one of Nazi Germany's most vaunted Strength-Through-Joy cruise liners, but by January 1945 she was one of the last ships to leave the Gulf of Danzig before the Russian armies swept in. She took on board a mixed cargo of refugees—fleeing peasants, fragmented army units, train and truck-loads of German wounded, the remnants of Prussian garrisons, members of the German Women's Naval Service and scores of SS officers and top-ranking Nazis. She was heavily overloaded, with an estimated 6,500 crammed on board, when she left Gotenhafen on a bitter January day.

Twelve miles off shore she was torpedoed. A minesweeper in the area, alert for further attack, could only pick up a small number of survivors. Panic broke out on board *Gustloff*, and there were scenes of appalling horror side by side with heroism and selflessness. An S.O.S. message brought the cruiser *Hipper* and an escorting destroyer to the rescue, but there was little they could do, and in the end only about 500 people survived from the *Gustloff*.

Measured in terms of loss of life, this was the greatest sea disaster ever recorded.

# The Damned Don't Drown

## The Sinking of the
## *Wilhelm Gustloff*

### A.V. SELLWOOD

NAVAL INSTITUTE PRESS

Annapolis, Maryland

BLUEJACKET BOOKS

Originally published in Great Britain by Allan Wingate
(Publishers) Ltd., London, in 1973. Reprinted by arrangement with
Mary Blyth Sellwood as heir to Arthur V. Sellwood.

First Bluejacket Books printing, 1996

Library of Congress Cataloging-in-Publication Data


Sellwood, A.V. (Arthur V.)
The damed don't drown : the sinking of the Wilhelm Gustloff/
A.V. Sellwood.
p.     cm. — (Bluejacket books)
Originally published: London : A. Wingate, 1973.
ISBN 1-55750-742-2 (pbk. : alk. paper)
1. Wilhelm Gustloff (Ship)   2. World War, 1939–1945—Naval operations—Submarine.
3. World War, 1939–1945—Naval operations, Russian.   I. Title.   II. Series.
D772.3.S43   1996
940.54′2174—dc20                                                95-36273


Printed in the United States of America on acid-free paper ∞

03   02   01   00   99   98   97   96     8  7  6  5  4  3  2  1

# Contents

# On a Personal Note

THE idea for this narrative of the events that led up to and accompanied the sinking of the German liner *Wilhelm Gustloff*, the biggest sea disaster of all time, was born in the streets of Berlin in 1948, at the time of the Russian blockade. It was there that, while on a journalistic assignment with the Allied Air Lift, I accidentally encountered relatives of one of the families lost in the tragedy, and first began to appreciate something of its mammoth scope.

Until then, to be candid, I had never heard of the *Gustloff* and knew very little of the Russo-German struggle in the Baltic. To me, as to most other Britons, war at sea had meant the battle against the U-boats in the North Atlantic, or MTB–E-boat duels fought off the coasts of Europe. It was not until some years after my encounter in Berlin, and at a time when I was researching my book *The Warring Seas*, that I met veterans of the 'Baltic' front and finally recognised the *Gustloff* sinking for what it was, introducing it to British readers in the shape of a feature for a national weekly newspaper.

Today, in *The Damned Don't Drown*, I have attempted a reconstruction of the tragedy that would have been impossible to manage without the help of others, among whom I would particularly mention :

Miss Ursula Kaltenbach, for her devoted work of research, and the translation of documents; Mr H. Filusch, of the staff of the German Naval Attaché in London; Mr Ulrich Ewart, London correspondent of *Bild-Zeitung*; Mr Roger Todd, of the *Daily Mirror* editorial staff, and the staffs of the libraries of the *Daily Mirror* and the Ministry of Defence.

To these friends, my warmest thanks.

A. V. SELLWOOD

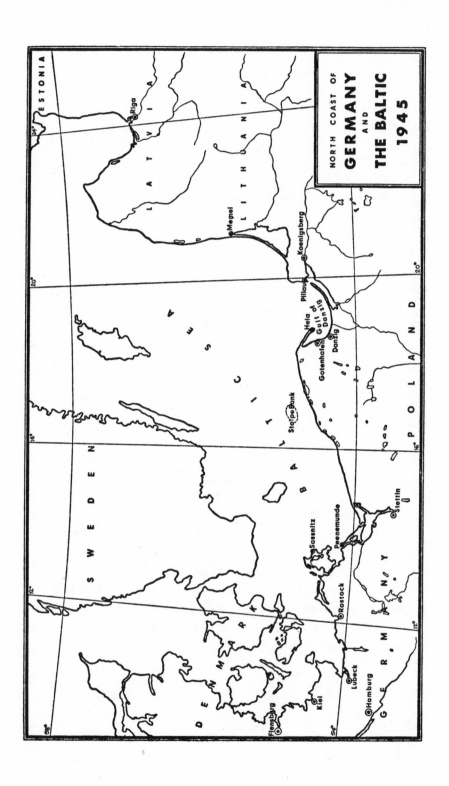

NORTH COAST OF
**GERMANY**
AND
**THE BALTIC**
**1945**

# The Damned . . .

As THE Waffen SS officer, death's head cap badge winking in the winter sun, approached the refugee ship alongside the naval jetty, the seaman at the foot of the gangplank felt his hackles rise.

Immaculately groomed, the new arrival looked so sure of himself and his right of precedence over the lesser breeds—the dejected civilians waiting in the queue—that he quite offended the sailor's sense of propriety.

To judge from the white markings on the black of his collar patch, the officer ranked no higher than lieutenant; but his arrogant air was worthy of a general.

'You'd think the SS comrades owned the sea as well as the land,' the seaman grumbled to his mate. 'Let's hope, for his sake, they've bloody well taught him to swim.'

It was indiscreet to utter such thoughts aloud, and he had not intended his subject to overhear them, but fortunately the officer appeared to bear no malice.

'Sailor,' he retorted with a tight-lipped smile, 'didn't anyone ever tell you that the damned don't drown!'

CHAPTER ONE

## *No Roses, No Wine*

JANUARY IN the naval base at Gotenhafen, a northern January with the sea lead-grey, its dullness broken only by the sharp glitter of ice. Oddly oppressive, it crouched almost unstirring against the shoreline, its wide carpet stretching northward to the dunes of the Hela Peninsula, sheltering the Gulf of Danzig from the Baltic.

To the crew of the concrete bunker guarding the approaches to the dockyard the scene was as comfortless as the dark snow-laden sky.

Moored alongside the jetty dividing the base from the inner harbour, or else anchored in line ahead along the length of the Roads, a drab-hued armada stretched as far as the eye could see. Ships of all shapes and sizes—from panzerschiff to Siebel ferry—they had little in common except the job that had brought them to this inhospitable haven, and the swastika insignia on the ensigns that hung limply at their sterns.

All through the previous week the ships had been assembling; each day increasing their numbers and variety of types. Together they now formed the greatest concourse of shipping the wide Gulf had ever seen: but they were not here to stay, and everyone knew it. Certainly the men of the bunker—sailors turned into soldiers at the stroke of the Fuehrer's baton—had few illusions as to the purpose of the fleet, or the factors that had impelled its concentration.

At first, the sounds of battle had been extremely hard to

hear; a weak pulse beating from the dark outline of the Samland and the depths of East Prussia, on the far side of the water.
But daily its rhythm, once wide-spaced and intermittent, had
been growing a little louder and becoming more closely knit
until now it was continuous and menacing, the thunder of a
rapidly nearing storm.

Fidgeting in their unfamiliar setting, the bunker crew considered the implications of the sound, and its correlation to the
mustered ships, with no enthusiasm and some depression, but
they kept their own counsel.

'Evacuation' was a dirty word, and to utter it could be
dangerous: for this was January—January '45—a time of re-
crimination, and uncovering of 'traitors'. The once glittering
New Order was drawing to its shabby and sombre close. The
enemies of the Reich were closing in for the kill.

In the West, the Ardennes offensive had been ground to a
permanent halt. Starved of fuel, bludgeoned from land and air,
the panzers that had spearheaded the Wehrmacht's last assault
could move no more. No longer free to prowl across the battle's
landscape—the scene that they had been so used to dominate—
the Tigers and Mark IVs were now mere monuments, so
many mastodons, to an era that was already past and gone:
landmarks for the Anglo-Saxons spilling across the frontiers en
route for Berlin.

But while things were bad enough on the Western Front, the
German defeat in the East was approaching the cataclysmic
—and even the seamen could see why.

Crack divisions urgently needed to defend Silesia, and reinforced for that purpose by drafts rushed in from the West and
Norway, had been switched by Hitler's orders to faraway
Budapest. An entire army group, aiming to stand firm on
shortened lines, had been sent instead to do battle in Lithuania:
and there it stayed, encircled, while the Russians hammered
down the gates of the Homeland.

'You will yield not an inch,' the Fuehrer had proclaimed,

when his generals had asked for permission to 're-arrange' the front. Short shrift had been given to those who had dared dissent, with consequences that were now all too plain to see.

The turn of the year had found less than fifty German divisions, many of them dangerously under strength, stretched taut along a line that reached from the Baltic coast to the heart of the Carpathians. Having tried to hold every place, they were strong in no place. Attempting to yield nothing, they were in danger of losing everything.

It was the thirteenth of January when Rokossovsky struck. . . .

Cracking the thin defences to the north of Warsaw, his armour swept the Polish plain, then switched to a forked offensive into Germany itself. With odds in his favour of seven to one in numbers of guns and men—and with nine tanks to every two deployed by the defenders—the outcome was never in doubt. One prong of the Russian advance was now stabbing deep into East Prussia, isolating its capital, historic Koenigsberg. The other was fast approaching Danzig Bay.

'And next it's the turn of us poor sods,' the sailors thought.


Seen from the wings of the spacious glass-enclosed bridge of the former passenger liner *Wilhelm Gustloff,* queening it over the lesser breeds alongside the naval jetty, Gotenhafen's prospects of surviving the new offensive were as bleak as the local weather.

Since the opening of the previous Russian onslaught, held only by superhuman effort in the Fall of '44, the base and neighbouring Danzig had been filling with the human flotsam thrown up by the tide of the Wehrmacht's retreat. But their numbers had been light compared with this latest influx: its size, and the diversity of its elements, epitomised by the untidy queues that, shepherded into the dockyard, had spilled out on to the quays to besiege the ships themselves.

Shawled peasant women in bewildered flight from primitive villages in Lithuania, sturdy 'settlers' displaced from the rich farmlands of the Ukraine, a hotch-potch of fragmented army units and Luftwaffe ground personnel—all these, and more, had converged on the Danzig bottleneck, crossroad for escapees from the East and embarkation point for the sea-route to the West.

Truckloads of mauled survivors from East Prussia's fallen fortresses . . . women and children by the thousand, evacuees from Danzig proper . . . a sprinkling of VIPs and officials of the Party . . . the multitudes of the dispossessed were looking to the ships as to so many Noah's Arks, their sole hope of refuge from the overwhelming flood.

Even a man equipped with the professional calm of Friederich Petersen, commanding the *Gustloff*, largest ark of all, found the view from the bridge almost unbearably depressing.

Up to a fortnight ago the base at Gotenhafen, formerly the Polish port of Gdynia, had been the safe and well-equipped nerve centre of the Navy's rescue operations in areas further east.

Riga . . . Memel . . . the Courland Peninsula . . . time and time again, the warships and transports had sallied forth from the Gulf to aid the defenders of these beleaguered 'laagers'. And time after time they had returned in modest triumph, laden with those they had snatched from the furnace of the battle. But today the place of refuge was itself becoming a 'pocket', and the civilians of the base were themselves about to flee.

Bowed and shabby, their skins almost translucent around the cheekbones, a long column of civilians had been set to work unloading a string of flat wagons, parked on the railway track flanking the road into the docks. Behind them, on a site where the caterpillar treads of tanks and SPs had churned the earth into black-brown porridge—extra filthy by its contrast with the snow—flak crews were busying themselves around a pair of

88's. The pale wood smoke from the fires of dejected soldiers, squatting on their hunkers in the slush, reeked sourly in the nostrils. 'The bitter stink of defeat', a thoughtful observer was later to describe it. The soldiers had a ruder word for it.

Forgotten were the heady days of 'liberation', when neighbouring Danzig City, festooned with flags, had 'come home to the Reich'. Gone for ever was the era of roses and champagne.


'They're all here,' said Petersen, turning his binoculars on the harbour. 'All here—all that is left of them!'

The pocket battleship *Lutzow*, the heavy cruiser *Admiral Hipper*, a light cruiser or two and half a dozen destroyers—nearly all that remained afloat of the Kriegsmarine's surface units had turned up for the big evacuation: the evacuation all knew to be imminent, but very few cared to own.

Daily the Reichsenders had been plugging the No Surrender theme. 'Hold the Flood Back!' had become the heroic exhortation of the hour. Slogans abounded on The Will to Victory. 'We will fight until five minutes past midnight,' the Fuehrer had proclaimed. Herr Himmler had taken effective steps to ensure the pledge was honoured by the public. The Reich of a Thousand Years had no use for 'weaklings and traitors'; for those who 'stood fast' victory was inevitable. With such a gospel being preached by the leaders of the faithful, who were mere naval officers to intrude a depressing note?

And yet, despite the efficiency of the regime's publicists in representing current setbacks as purely temporary in their nature, there were portents to the contrary that just could not be ignored. One such was the recent voyage of the *Emden*, escaping down the Ship Canal from beleagured Koenigsberg, and thence via the Gulf of Danzig to the West. The *Emden*'s hazardous trip, and the reason inspiring it, had been treated as top secret at the time, yet somehow word of it had got round the Fleet in a matter of hours, arousing mixed feelings of pride and melancholy, and the reflection that it had done more to reveal the leadership's real thoughts about the future than anything yet contributed by official sources.

The cruiser had been undergoing an engine overhaul in the East Prussian capital when the Red Army had commenced its attack on the outer suburbs and the city's fall had seemed imminent. No dockyard workers were available—all had been called up for service with the Volkssturm—and the ship's company had to load her with stores and fuel the hard way. With cranes and gantries unworkable, they had to do everything by hand, and do it against the most disconcerting background. The Russians had opened a heavy artillery bombardment, and the docks were also the targets of air attack. Yet when their labours were successful, and the ship made ready for sea, the tired men were amazed to hear that she was forbidden to leave. The elderly *Emden*—a 'sitting duck' if ever there was one—must stay in the dock, already flooded, to await 'special cargo'.

'Special cargo'? To keep a light cruiser standing-by in such critical conditions the cargo, all hands agreed, must indeed be 'special', and speculation was rife as to its nature. A secret weapon, maybe, moved from a threatened site? One of those 'weapons of annihilation' promised by the Fuehrer, which would turn the tide and bring Germany to victory? But even the wildest of rumours fell short of the reality. When the anxiously-awaited shipment eventually arrived, in a heavily guarded truck convoy travelling at dead of night, it was found to consist of two coffins!

One of them contained the remains of Field Marshal von Hindenburg, the hero of World War I, the victor of Tannenberg and 'saviour of East Prussia'. The other held the body of the old warrior's wife.

Reverently carried on to the deck of the cruiser by their soldier escorts, the coffins were surrounded by a barricade of floats to prevent them from being swept overboard, while a guard of honour hurriedly improvised from the *Emden's* crew

presented arms in the snow-flecked blackness of the winter
night, and the couple's son—a serving army officer on special
leave from the front—arrived to bid his parents a filial farewell.

Then, and then only, did the cruiser commence her voyage,
with officers and ship's company alike both awed by the
solemnity of the occasion and oppressed by its significance;
sombre in the extreme.

The coffins had been retrieved from the hallowed resting
place that had so often been the goal of German pilgrims in the
heyday of the Reich—the towering memorial that had been
erected on the scene of the Field Marshal's former triumph. The
Hindenburgs had left Tannenberg, because Tannenberg had
fallen. . . .

In later years, a German writer was to comment on the
emotion aroused in the Navy by this eerie but strangely moving
event : 'Was it not symbolic of the last month of the war—the
victor of 1915 fleeing from the victor of 1945 ?'

Captain Petersen, for one, would not have considered the
parallel unduly overdrawn. The world that had been Germany
was falling apart, and all that the Navy could do about it was
to pick up some of the bits. Biggest ship in the harbour, the
*Wilhelm Gustloff* would be expected to pick up more than most.


Even merchant service veterans of the *Gustloff* in peacetime
found it difficult at times to remember the way the ship had
looked when, painted dazzling white overall, she had first
steamed for the sunshine in the autumn of '37.

The *Gustloff* had so much changed her role and coat in meeting the war's demands that their uncertainty was fairly under-
standable, yet not even the regulation Kriegsmarine livery of
grey could completely conceal the distinctive 'liner' stamp of
her long and graceful hull.

Nearly 650 feet long, and displacing 25,000 tons, the *Wilhelm
Gustloff* was no giant, not when compared with the great

Cunarders and their rival from France, the *Normandie*. But
measured by Baltic standards she was indeed a fish among the
minnows. No competitor for the coveted Blue Riband—her
speed was relatively modest—she was the product of a nice
alliance between the profit motive and power politics that was
a model of the way the Third Reich transacted business. In a
partnership of self-interest between shipbuilders and regime,
she made money for the one and kudos for the other. More, she
won friends and influenced people.

With a passenger list of 'approved' workers, carried on highly
publicised holidays subsidised by the State, the *Wilhelm Gustloff*
was designed as a 'People's Ship', a floating platform for the
Goebbels propaganda machine and the 'radical' image he pro-
jected of the Party. Cruising in ocean playgrounds hitherto
reserved for millionaires, and linked with the organisation
Strength Through Joy, she was to be, as a sponsor frankly put
it, 'a standard-bearer on the oceans of the National Socialist
Idea!'

As the thirties drew to their close, the *Gustloff* was more than
living up to such pious expectations. During her peacetime
career, brief though it was, she was as much an instrument of
national policy as the largest warship engaged in showing the
flag. On extravagantly publicised voyages to foreign ports, the
ship and her sisters were soon established as floating showpieces
for the regime, their activities heaping coals of fire on the heads
of those who had denounced it as the creature of reaction. With
her passengers so obviously enjoying themselves, and her hospitality—on a scale that was truly lavish—dispensed to all who
came visiting, it was obvious that the New Germany could not
be quite so black as it was painted. Somehow even the swastika
appeared to lose its menace when perched on the top of a
pleasure steamer's funnel.

To Petersen, meditating on the task ahead, that palmy period
seemed a century ago. The cocktail parties and the 'Festing'
sessions . . . the deckgames and the visitors' nights . . . all these

were past, and would never be seen again. For the *Gustloff*, as for others, the Good Life was over.

With 30mm and 20mm light flak guns pointing skywards from her stern, and a miniature mountain of rubber floats secured abaft her funnel, it was hard to credit that less than six years had passed since the ship had begun to adjust herself to the needs of war. In the Kaiser's day, she might have been designed with an eye to her future use as a commerce raider. Decks would have been strengthened, gun-mounts installed, provision made for fuel storage during far-reaching cruises. But in an age when maritime aircraft and the magic-eye of radar had added greatly to the risks of detection her service had been in a less dramatic field.

When choosing its auxiliary cruisers for World War II, the Kriegsmarine plumped for ships of medium size and nondescript appearance : ships that could be easily disguised as peaceful merchantmen and reveal their true colours only when the time was opportune for action. The *Gustloff*'s lines being too distinctive for such subterfuge, it was left to others to play the raider role. Thus, while the chameleon-like *Atlantis* (Ship Sixteen) and a handful of other converted freighters forayed against the enemy's world-wide sealanes, the Queen of the Strength Through Joy fleet was confined to the Baltic.

Requisitioned shortly after the outbreak of hostilities, she was later classed as a Lazaretschiff—a floating military hospital. Simultaneously she became an accommodation ship for off-duty U-boat crews. Ethically dubious, this duality of role? Justified by the exigencies of the time, the planners said. Bombing raids and allied advances by land took a heavy toll of shore barracks, and of hospitals too. To a naval administration desperately seeking living space for its personnel, the *Gustloff* was an attractive alternative to fixed-site shore installations of dubious viability. Later still, with Germany's fortunes about to reach rock-bottom, the *Willi G* (as she had come to be known) was called on to meet yet another urgent need : as submarine training ship, and depot for that odd improvisation, the Naval Division, composed of seamen made 'surplus' by cuts in the ship-building programme.

Even now, despite the many structural changes imposed by such demands on her hospitality, it was impossible to disguise the ship's proud lineage. Viewed from the jetty she was very much the Navy workhorse, with ABs in fatigue gear loading shells and collapsible dinghies, or cleaning the barrels of the guns that protruded over the rim of her cliff-like hull. However much her purpose had altered with the years, and however drab and wrinkled her once-immaculate paintwork, the *Gustloff*, it was agreed, was nevertheless a lady. If her brilliance had faded, like a duchess fallen on hard times, she still had her admirers. Kapitaen Friederich Petersen was one of them.

For what ship but the ex-liner *Willi G* could have adapted herself so rapidly, and so well, to the role now wished upon her : the latest and most demanding of them all? 'You'll be carrying lots of wounded, and a host of refugees,' they'd said, when Petersen had paid a call on Base HQ. 'Your ship must be ready to sail at a moment's notice.'

Prewar, the *Gustloff* had accommodation for a maximum of 1,800 passengers. Now, from what her Captain could make of the figures they gave him, nearly 4,000 lives would be entrusted to her care.

Only five days had passed since that directive from the Base planners. Into those five days had been telescoped what normally would have been the work of a month. Apart from a detachment selected for the active U-boat fleet, the 2,000 or so young sailors for whom the *Gustloff* had been home had to be put ashore, where they were immediately organised for the land defence of the city. Next, provision had to be made to receive, feed—and clothe if need be—the refugees who would be replacing them. In itself the switch had posed quite serious problems, but Petersen had contrived to take them in his stride.

To impose some sort of order on the muddled crowds on the quayside and ensure the right priorities were observed on embarkation, he had set the ship's printing press to work producing boarding passes. Forms were prepared that would record passengers' next of kin. Then, aiming at keeping confusion to a minimum in what to most of the intake would be a completely alien environment, he reopened and staffed the enquiry bureau used by the *Gustloff* during her peacetime cruising and 'signposted' the various areas of the ship. Members of the ship's company were detailed to act as guides, and some were even appointed baby-minders. Permits for extra rations were prepared, for issue to toddlers. Precious milk was scrounged for them, and, astonishingly, a little chocolate too. Even the news that the local hospitals were sending a consignment of pregnant women, most of them approaching their time, had failed to daunt the stalwarts of the *Gustloff*. Promptly they had partitioned off part of the sun-deck, and turned it into a maternity ward. 'Das kann doch einen Seemann nicht erschüttern' ('But that won't shake a sailor!') was the slogan of the hour.

What *had* disturbed the Captain's confidence—and continued to fidget him now—was the uncertain state of the ship's engines. Could they, so long unused, be relied upon to cope with the demands that a high-speed run through the gale-swept Baltic would make on them. To trace and remedy deficiencies, the engine-room staff were kept working round the clock. But of even greater concern was the inadequacy of the lifeboats. When the order had been given to prepare for sea, the *Willi G*'s davits were almost empty. Not one of her impressive quota of large motor-driven boats remained aboard: all of them had been commandeered for ships on operations. A 'floating barracks', it was said, had no need of such refinements. Now, with the 'barracks' about to embark a host of helpless non-combatants and take them through the mine-infested sea, Petersen was acutely aware of the seriousness of his loss.

He had shopped around in quest of replacements for the boats, but the best he had been able to obtain were a number of naval whalers, usually employed in giving young recruits their basic training in seamanship. For such a role they were eminently suitable—sturdy craft with good sea-keeping qualities. But they were dependent on oars for their propulsion, and offered their occupants little shelter against the weather. Certainly they wouldn't be the easiest of refuges for unskilled landsmen, let alone women and children. And also, of course, there were the wounded to worry about. . . .

## CHAPTER TWO

## Sour Sweat of Fear

THE FIRST of the wounded had already come aboard, men from a crowded hospital train that had pulled into the sidings of the Oxenholte station only a few hundred yards from the *Gustloff*'s berth. Now they were being followed by a second batch, from a long convoy of field ambulances, supplemented by commandeered civilian cars and trucks. The sailors, all banter ceased, watched their arrival in a sort of awed silence, and then went down the gangplank to lend a helping hand.

Blanket-swathed and inert as logs on the stretchers that bore them, or else, supported by crutches, stumbling slowly up the side of the ship with faces as grey and dirty as their tattered, mud-caked field overcoats, the wounded looked to the refuge of the *Gustloff* with the eyes of dead men, awakening to life. Most of them were casualties from East Prussia but there were others among them who had been wounded in actions even nearer home. The local Volkssturm were receiving their baptism of blood.

As the process of embarking the wounded got under way a certain restiveness became apparent among the civilian by-standers—a restiveness that struck responsive chords among the seamen, occupied though they were with the task in hand. No psychologist was necessary to explain its cause : the cause was obvious to any with eyes to see. Patient though they might be—and some were almost stoical—the victims of the battle were branded not only by their wounds, but also by the iron of defeat.

Even the most hardened of the *Gustloff*'s officers felt sickness gripe at their stomachs as they saw the physical condition of these men from the front. But almost equally were they sickened by the implications of the retreating tide of which the wounded were part. How long before the streets of Gotenhafen witnessed at close range the carnage of battle? Few could avoid the thought, or its grim corollary: that the day of the Third Reich was ending here as it had ended elsewhere, and that no sacrifice, however great, could do more than delay by a fraction the coming of the night.

However, despite such sombre reflections—off-shoots of the sense of doom which in varying degrees oppressed them all— the seamen still contrived to keep their feelings well buttoned-up. Certainly they did not allow them to stray to the point where they interfered with the job in hand. This, contrary to expectation, was soon proceeding fairly smoothly; a phenomenon for which most of the credit was due to the ship's lift. The *Gustloff*'s large passenger lift, a relic of her ocean-liner past, had inevitably been derided as a luxury by those pursuing their calling in 'real' warships; but for the wounded it was proving a major boon. Many of them were being moved into the wards on the sun-deck, next door to the improvised 'maternity wing', and accommodation had been found for the others in the decks below. But the journey inflicted on them only the minimum of additional discomfort. The agonies that would have accompanied the jolting progress of their stretchers on successive flights of stairs were mercifully spared them by the lift, and for this not only they, but their hosts as well, were duly grateful.

All the same, even while they found time to indulge in brief self-congratulation at the outcome of the most delicate of transfers, the men of the *Gustloff* viewed the future through no rose-tinted spectacles. Soldiers, even wounded soldiers, were disciplined in their responses to danger. But how would the frightened civilians who now thronged the wharfside, settle in the unfamiliar routine of the crowded ship? How well would they brace themselves against the hazards of the voyage ahead?

For Ruth Fleischer, the silhouette of the *Wilhelm Gustloff*, looming monstrous over the quayside now that the tide was high, was not quite the lodestone it was to other holders of the coveted 'sailing permit', comrades in flight though all of them were. She had been badly scared—who hadn't been?—by the rumours that had been sweeping the Base for days: rumours that Gotenhafen's fall was imminent, with rape and carnage bound to follow. Nor could she have denied that at times her fears had bordered on abject terror, conceal it though she might try. Her letters home to her parents in the 'safe' South had been cheerful to excess; but the cheer was forced, high-pitched to the point where it bordered on hysteria.

Yet however great the anxieties that afflicted her, Ruth had one very good reason for being part-sorry to go: she would have to leave her husband behind. For young Lieutenant Fleischer, on active service with the Kriegsmarine, the *Gustloff* could be no vehicle of escape. Now, while her companions were gratefully trudging up the gangplank, Frau Fleischer found herself transferring her gaze from her immediate surroundings to the fleet that had mustered outside the harbour, focusing eventually on the pocket-battleship *Lutzow*.

Lean as a hungry wolf—and not half as handsome—the *Lutzow* was no obvious magnet for ship-lovers, yet the girl gazed at her affectionately, as if in tender reminiscence, and continued to do so until a guard moved her on. Somewhere aboard the grim panzerschiff was the husband who had ordered her to safety; the safety that he himself was denied. She had been married to him for a few hours short of five days.

For sixteen-year-old Eva Luck, accompanying her mother and elder sister aboard the *Gustloff*, there was also a certain regret at the need to leave the city. Even her excitement at the

prospect that her father would be waiting to greet the ship on
its arrival was dampened by the fact that the Gulf and its surroundings had been home to her for as long as she could remember, and she could envisage no other. True that, in recent
days, the secure scene of her childhood had collapsed around
her, but the catastrophe had seemed unreal, a nightmare from
which she would eventually awaken. Her mother knew better.
This was the second time in a quarter-century that, at short
notice, Frau Luck had had to leave everything and flee towards
the West : and on each occasion she had fled from the same foe.
When a youngster, she had reached the Gulf from Lithuania
where the White armies were in retreat before the Bolsheviks.
Yes, Frau Luck had seen it all before. Even so, she had to con-
cede, she was fortunate by comparison with others caught up
in this current tragedy. Her husband—himself a former refugee
—was serving in the West. Every mile the *Gustloff* made would
bring him nearer. . . .

For the ship's company the day continued to be one of in-
tensive labour. The *Willi G* was filling so rapidly with passengers
that wherever you went, the watch complained, you'd be sure
to find one of them under your feet. And adding to the volume
and diversity of their chores was Petersen's obsessive concern
about the lifeboats. Not only was he dissatisfied with their type
and performance; he was also worried about their deficiency
in numbers. Should the ship manage to obtain her full com-
plement of boats there would be room inside them for only a
quarter of her anticipated passengers.

To help fill the gap, working parties were sent in search of
additional floats and dinghies, a mission in which they displayed both energy and resourcefulness. By requisitioning,
cajolery—and, so it was whispered, downright thieving—the
'Gustloffs' achieved a quite astonishing result. By the end of their
labours they had collected sufficient collapsibles to carry 5,000
people. Yet Petersen still remained unsatisfied. The new craft,
though very useful, were no real substitute for the *Gustloff*'s

missing lifeboats. Rafts and floats would be terribly vulnerable to the blows of the Baltic winter, particularly when the bulk of the people they would be called upon to carry would be composed of the old, the feeble and the sick.

Frau Bendrich, with two small children, one under each arm. . . . Another woman with a family of four—like so many steps of stairs from the age of six downwards. . . . Nearly a score of pregnant mothers, arriving at the dockside in ambulances. . . . And a group of violated teenage girls, raped by the Russians during the previous autumn and under medical treatment ever since. . . . Should the ship's luck fail, such passengers as these were unlikely to survive.

Should the ship's luck fail? The mind boggled at the prospect, and its horrific implications. 'Failure' aboard the *Gustloff* could escalate into catastrophe. It would be almost impossible for the crew to control such vast numbers of frightened people. Even if, against all possibility, the evacuees remained amenable to discipline, the scene would be completely chaotic. The crowds would get in each other's way, and the way of the seamen too. The *Gustloff* would be no *Birkenhead*!

However, as more and then more of her passengers came aboard, the men of the ship tried to thrust from their minds the thought of such a dreadful contingency. So far the Russians had not been notable for their prowess afloat and there was little reason to suppose that the situation had changed. Besides, there would be a naval escort for the *Gustloff* during the night, and air cover would be provided from dawn. More difficult to dismiss was the fear of her being caught in harbour. A hit by a shell or a bomb would turn the packed ship into a shambles. High time she got started, the seamen thought.

Another day limped by, with the *Gustloff* still in harbour. Instead of receiving her sailing orders the ship was directed to embark yet another load of civilian refugees: prominent 'locals' and folk on trek (one of the euphemisms of the age) from the frontiers of East Prussia. By the time this new intake had come aboard even the companionways had to be used as living quarters. But still they kept her dallying beside the harbour wall. As the hours passed even Petersen's façade of confidence began to crack. When the devil would Base allow him to get under way?

By now the sound of the guns was frighteningly loud. Quite obviously the front had drawn much closer. Earlier, the noise had been that of heavy artillery, but today could be heard the unmistakable snarl of the 'pianolas'—the dreaded Russian multi-barrelled mortars. If the ship didn't get away soon she would be staying put for ever! Yet around and aboard the *Gustloff* incidents were occurring that would have seemed farcical had the situation been less grave—fierce discussions among the passengers about the occupancy of cabins, petty squabbles concerning precedence and rank. Of these, perhaps the silliest was the Carpet Affair. This arose after a group of Party officials accompanied by their wives had debouched from a trio of shining black Mercedes and approached the gangplank. The women sported heavy furs and expensive jewellery. The men, with one exception—resplendent in full uniform and glittering jackboots—were in 'civilian' suits and overcoats. They were followed by orderlies carrying suitcases.

'Some people have it soft!' the sailors grumbled, viewing the procession with disfavour, but their envious annoyance quickly changed to stupefaction when the orderlies, having deposited the cases on the deck, returned to the cars to collect a pair of rolled carpets.

*Carpets!*

'I'm sorry, gentlemen,' said the officer on duty, 'but you will have to leave this heavy stuff behind you. Only personal luggage can be brought aboard. Captain's orders...'

That did it.

While the uniformed leader of the group appeared to accept the situation, two of the other officials objected, backed loyally

in their protests by their wives. They were 'privileged', they
claimed, and were not to be intimidated by the Navy's insistence
on Red Tape.

'Captain's orders. . . .' the Lieutenant doggedly repeated, but
they paid little attention to him. He was 'obstructionist', they
claimed. He should use his initiative. Orders were meant to be
broken!

At this, he hit back. 'I see that the Herren are in civilians,'
he said meaningfully, then, turning to his men, he added with
mock seriousness: 'You can observe that the comrades have
done their bit for Citizen's Sacrifice Day!'

There was a guffaw of delight, quickly suppressed. The thrust
was based on a joke widely circulated by the Underground,
so it was wise to keep one's appreciation pitched on a modest
key. But they all knew what their officer was getting at. Perhaps
never before had so many calls for sacrifice been made as now,
when the Reich was slipping from disaster into death, but the
sacrifices had come mainly from the rank and file: the behaviour of executives had left much to be desired. However (so
the 'joke' ran) the current call had met with an enthusiastic
response from these local leaders. Designed to encourage gifts of
clothing to ease the acute textile shortage, it had given them a
chance to prove not only their patriotism, but also their skill
in the art of self-survival. Swastika armbands, brown shirts
and riding breeches, glossy jackboots and stormtrooper caps—
all were being 'sacrificed' to the street collectors as the Russian
advance drew nearer. Never before had so many been so eager
to don unobtrusive mufti.

'I see that the Herren are in civilian clothes. . . .' It was a
daring comment to have made in the prevailing climate, and
reactions were angry.

'He has insulted my husband,' cried the wife of one of the
officials, appealing to the uniformed leader.

But the latter, with a complacent glance at his own immacu-
late turnout, merely answered with rare equanimity: 'We are

guests aboard this ship, my dear, and we must do what the
Lieutenant says. . . .'

The latter smiled relievedly as the frustrated officials, leaving the carpets on the quayside, clumped angrily past him and,
still protesting, vanished into the interior of the ship. Lucky, he
reflected, that their leader had been wearing his full regalia :
luckier still that he had found the jibe about 'civilians' flatter-
ing to his ego. Still, as the veteran *Gustloff* Petty Officer slyly
suggested, 'I'd watch it if I were you, sir. They don't like being
beaten.' Somewhat wearily, the Lieutenant turned to greet the
next arrivals. Yes, one could over-reach oneself, and push one's
luck too far.

After this sharp exchange with the privileged of the Party, it
did the 'Gustloffs' a lot of good to see the 'helfs' arrive. These
fresh-looking young women of the Marinehelferinnen, Germany's nearest—though still remote—equivalent to the Royal
Navy's WRNS, paraded in good order and with quite a flourish.
Their forage caps set jauntily on their highly feminine hair-
styles, and their short skirts swinging provocatively as they
marched towards the ship, they attracted not only wolf whistles
and cheers, but also a buzz of admiration and respect. It was
as though the helfs were cocking a snook at the miserable dockyard scene.

True that most of them were drawn from Base HQ and had
had the time—and facilities—for making themselves look
attractive. Even so, they made everyone feel better. Who could
have guessed, as they passed on to their quarters—the drained
swimming-pool on E-deck, seven levels from the boats—that
their youth and vigour was to be soon extinguished? The
Helferinnen—nearly 300 of them—had less than three days to
live.


The 28th dawned uneasily, with near-panic spreading among
the crowds along the wharves, and influencing in turn the

crowds aboard the ships. Much of this was due to the evidence of their own eyes and ears: the misfortunes of the hour were all too plain to see. But it was also attributable to the latest arrivals in the queue. The newcomers seemed obliged to excel each other in the stories they told of the horrors they had witnessed, and even the strongest 'loyalist' began to waver when confronted by their appearance of absolute dejection and defeat.

By now it had become obvious that Petersen's plans for an orderly embarkation were in danger of total breakdown. Scores of people were coming aboard who had no claim, save compassion, for a ticket, and the sailors were turning a blind eye to the influx, lacking the will of iron needed to drive these unfortunates away. But there were others, probably hundreds, in excess of the 4,000 total originally called for, who had arrived with the blessing of HQ. Between them, they hourly increased the strains imposed on the *Gustloff*'s administration, and complicated still further the problem of maintaining discipline.

In the early afternoon, while the harassed Petersen was considering suggestions from his officers to approach Base with a request for permission to sail, his worries were increased by the arrival of a fresh batch of refugees, this time by train. As the battered old locomotive, her soot-encrusted hide pitted with the scars of near-misses, towed her long string of freight wagons and tank transporters into the Oxenholte station, the watch raised an ironic cheer. But then, as she came to a stop, and blew off, as though expiring, a huge cloud of steam, their irony changed to alarm. The train was disgorging people . . . hordes of people . . . ten times the numbers of people they'd have thought it possible for her to carry.

'There seemed to be thousands of them . . . men, women and children . . . we could not imagine how a single train had housed such a vast multitude,' a *Gustloff* seaman later recalled. 'Then suddenly, we realised that the whole mass was beginning to run . . . worst of all, it was running to us!'

Yes, they certainly ran, those fugitives from ruin . . . ran
with their heads and shoulders crouched, as if under shellfire,
and with a mixture of terror and hope reflected on every face.
They had seen everything—*everything*—in the course of their
flight from the East. In the *Gustloff* and her sisters, they felt,
lay their only hope. They ran as if yards, not miles, lay between
them and the Reds—as if the Hounds of Hell were at their
backs.

Swiftly recovering from their astonishment, the ship's officers
cracked out orders to halt the onrush. Sailors dashed on deck
to reinforce the guards on the gangplank. The cordon of police
on the quayside intervened, riot sticks flying. But it was a good
quarter of an hour before the folk from the train were
restrained sufficiently for them to be marshalled into some sort
of order, to wait their turn in the queue.

'The fright of those people was really terrible [to quote the
seaman again] and gave us a very alarming insight into the sort
of thing they were experiencing up at the Front. Certainly it
made the statements of the Party look pretty sick. . . .'


'You must fight on, no matter where, and in no matter what
circumstances, until final victory crowns our efforts,' Adolf
Hitler had declared in a New Year's Eve message to the German
people. It was only the second time he had addressed them
since the Bomb Plot of the previous July, and his speech was
richly larded (as before) with allusions to 'traitors' and their
fates.

'The sick and infirm and the otherwise dispensible,' he said,
'must work to the last ounce of their strength. The horrible fate
suffered by tens and hundreds of thousands of our countrymen
in the east, with all its tribulations and trials, will eventually
be mastered. Whoever stabs us in the back will die a wretched
death!'

Although the Fuehrer's promises—'Total victory will be

ours'—were by now somewhat suspect, there was little doubt
of his continuing capacity to implement his threats. Days after
the speech, the S.S. Colonel and Chief of Police from Bromberg
was executed. 'He forgot his duty,' it was laconically announced.
Nor had he been the only high official to rue the hour when his
heart had dared to soften at the sufferings of his people. Bromberg's Civil Administrator, the District Administrator, and the
local District Leader, had also paid a very heavy price. Although spared from death, they were deprived of all civil rights
and then sent to the dreaded penal battalions.

Another day's wait in harbour added to the *Gustloff*'s many
crosses, the dark suspicion that the delay might have a sinister
motivation. The ship was abuzz with unhealthy rumours of
conditions in the interior, rumours of wholesale defections and
summary punishments. While the facts were bad enough in
themselves, they were exaggerated a hundredfold as the hours
went by, with effects on morale that were predictably damaging.
Fear of the enemy—the uniformed foreigner—was something
that could vanish in the euphoria created by even a local
success, but fears of an enemy within, working his malevolent
will in stealth, were not half so easily dispersed. The feeling that
they could not trust their own was new to the refugees, but
steadily took roots. Growing more and more restless at the inexplicable way in which they were being kept chained to the
port's unhealthy environment, they credited the most implau-
sible canards, gave credence to the wildest bits of gossip.

On the bridge, the officers waited anxiously—more anxiously
than ever before—for the order from headquarters that could
end this nightmare of waiting. Every hour of it would bring
about a further deterioration in the spirit of the ship's company;
bring closer to breaking point the over-stretched nerves of the
fugitive civilians. And not only the civilians. . . .

B

## CHAPTER THREE

## *'Happy Voyage!'*

'ARE THEY out of their minds at HQ, holding us back in harbour? When the hell will they give us the word to go? I can't keep my poor devils living on hope for much longer. . . .'

The army doctor was disgruntled and worried, and small wonder at that. To get his convoy of badly wounded soldiers into Gotenhafen, departure point for the evacuation fleet, had required the performance of near-miracles of ingenuity and energy, and he'd been liberal in his outlay, never sparing himself. Advised that speed was the essence—the ships couldn't wait, he'd been told—he had driven himself hard, and his charges hard as well. Now, after forty-eight hours spent in waiting, he was experiencing to the full the frustrating anti-climax of his effort. The damned ships were showing not the slightest sign of movement, and someone should explain what the delay was all about. Yet up on the bridge they seemed to know no more than he did.

The doctor's disenchantment was not unique. Petersen, though he tried not to show it, shared it to the full. He had still received no information from the shore on the sailing time, or orders for the ship, not even a word to say that points he had made earlier on his accommodation plans were being considered. Nothing at all had come from Base. Nothing but silence. Uneasily he and his officers had discussed the ever-lengthening tally of would-be passengers, but had come to no positive decision as to what was to be done about it. Someone must make

34

it clear that a halt would have to be called to the embarkation, but none of them relished the prospect of doing so. The job of telling these unfortunates that the *Gustloff* must be barred to them in order to facilitate the chances of escape for those already aboard would be a heart-breaking chore. Better by far for authority to do the deed itself. But 'authority' did not oblige. Although the situation was becoming almost increasingly explosive the *Gustloff*, so it seemed, had been left to carry the can.

The first wave of fugitives had posed few problems except those associated with their accommodation. But some of their successors presented problems by the score. Not only were they scared stiff, they were resentful as well: jealous of the 'privileged' priority passengers and prone to exhibitions of hysteria and rage. Soon, the officers argued, they would not be able to control them. The time might come when the ship herself would be endangered, maybe even over-run.

At last, exposed to so much pressure for information, Petersen felt that he could no longer maintain the reserve considered appropriate to his role and content himself with merely awaiting orders. He must force the issue. . . .

'*Wilhelm Gustloff* with 4,000 passengers aboard requests permission to leave.'

'*Requests* permission'? The signal was more of a demand than a request, and was blunt to the point of rudeness. But having swallowed the camel, so to speak, why should Petersen strain at a gnat? At least this initiative should provoke an early reply. It did, but it wasn't very much to his liking.

'You will continue to embark refugees,' came the terse answer. 'Transport *Deutschland* has 8,000 aboard.'

The rebuke was plain. If the *Deutschland* could carry 8,000 why couldn't the *Wilhelm Gustloff*? Was the ship turning yellow, or something?

At Ost-See they had more sympathy with Petersen's predica-
ment than was apparent from the wording of the signal. Sympathy, but little thought—or hope—of easing the causes of his
discontent.

The pace and style of the Russian breakthrough on land had
not only thrown the whole of the Eastern territories into complete confusion; it was also likely to upset the balance of seapower in the area, even though this was as yet appreciated by
only a few. Until the Red Army's offensive, the heavy ships of
the so-called 'Training Squadron'—surely the most understated
weapon in the armoury of the Reich—had reigned almost
supreme, indeed almost unchallenged, throughout the Baltic.
As from now, things could be very different. Since the heady
initial successes of 'Barbarossa', launched to the accompaniment of trumpet fanfares in the summer of '41, Gotenhafen had
been the lynch-pin of Germany's exercise of seapower in the
Baltic. From the moment the place had first been incorporated
in the Reich, following the collapse of Poland, its complex of
docks and port installations had been continually broadened
and strengthened until, together with its neighbour and former
rival the city of Danzig, it was comparable with the great
western bases of Kiel and Wilhelmshaven. Thanks to Gotenhafen the Kriegsmarine had come to dominate the Eastern
Sea, its sway extending to the direct approaches to Leningrad
and, seemingly, a thing of permanency. Even the inroads of the
Western bombers, and Soviet aircraft from newly conquered
bases, had done little to change this reassuring picture : damage
had been slight when compared with the havoc inflicted, say,
on Hamburg. But so much had come to depend on Gotenhafen's continuing viability that, should it fall, the consequences
would reach the catastrophic. The Fleet would be forced to pull
back to Western bases, and the German garrisons still fighting
on in the north-east could no longer receive the prompt and
effective support of naval gunnery, engaging Russian tank for-
mations at ranges of up to twenty miles. Nor would there be the

steady two-way traffic, supplying food and ammunition on the
one hand, and evacuating wounded on the other, that had been
functioning since the time of the first Russian offensive into
Europe, in the summer of '44. Instead, soldiers and civilians
alike, their communications would be entirely dependent on a
sea lane highly vulnerable to air, mine and torpedo attack, and
with its terminal, hundreds of miles away, under the bombardment of R.A.F. and American bombers. Should Gotenhafen
fall, the work of the Fleet would be doubled, and its effective-
ness halved. At all costs the place must be defended and held.

But perhaps even more threatening to this objective than the
direct impact of the Red Army on the Gulf's defences was the
result of the indirect pressure exerted by the Russian offensive
—the mass entry into the area of the people displaced from the
lost territories. Already the small port of Pillau on the far side
of the Gulf was virtually unusable, so tightly was it crammed
with evacuees, and Gotenhafen must somehow be spared a
similar fate. Mouths to feed are liabilities in a siege, and the
extra mouths in the threatened zone could be numbered in
millions. The *Gustloff* must lift as many as she could, even
though her best efforts would be only a drop in the ocean compared with the magnitude of the crisis.

The Base planners' natural desire to load the ship to the
maximum was by no means the only factor that was keeping
her so long in harbour. Circumstances were changing daily, and
policies changing with them. Say there should be a sudden
switch in the evacuation programme, and the 'refugee transport' be required to carry soldiers instead? Fantastic though it
might seem, this eventuality could not be entirely ruled out.
Ships were in short supply for moving civilians *out* of Gotenhafen, but they were also in short supply for bringing soldiers
*in*. As recently as the 22nd of the month, Grand Admiral
Doenitz, as C-in-C Navy, had reported to Hitler that there was
only three weeks' supply of coal available for 'sea transport',
and only ten days' supply for the railways needed to carry the

troops up to the front. Bearing in mind the calls made on the
Navy to transport and escort army units from places as far
apart as Norway and the Courland Peninsula, there was no recourse but for the coal-burning craft to 'abandon the evacuation of refugees'.

The Fuehrer had agreed with this grim summary of the
situation, and had endorsed the lines of its Draconian solution.
'Coal supplies,' he had ordered, 'must be reserved for military
operations alone and must not be used for evacuating refugees.'
At the same time, however, he had obtained Doenitz's promise
that the Navy would 'do everything possible' to help embark
those unfortunates 'on oil-burning ships which can temporarily
be spared from other operations', a promise that had given the
*Gustloff* her existing role, and had been responsible for the lifting of over 62,000 civilians from East and West Prussia in the
course of just five days. But on the 28th there was an apparent
change of emphasis in the Grand Admiral's thinking. 'The
C-in-C Navy', recorded the minutes of the day's Fuehrer Conference, 'informs the Fuehrer that the refugees can be evacuated
by sea *only in so far as this operation does not affect the transfer of fighting forces from Kurland and Norway.*'

Say that the *Gustloff* was called on to assist with such a 'transfer'? Small thanks would anyone get if the ship, when urgently
required to rush soldiers to the defence of the city, were to be
found, instead, halfway to the West, crowded with citizens who
had managed to get out!


The night of the 29th/30th was sheer hell aboard the *Gustloff*.
Arriving by boat from the far side of the Gulf—rumour was
that the overland route had been completely severed—came
yet another batch of refugees, and following them yet another
load of wounded. Orders had been issued to keep the companionways clear, but with such numbers to contend with this
had proved quite impossible. Even the routine handling of the

ship was placed in jeopardy by the exiles, preventing the free passage of the crew, and nothing short of violence could budge them. Officers and men proceeding to their duties had to push their way through crowds of people and their personal belongings—people who everywhere accosted them with questions they could not answer. How far off were the Bolsheviks? Just what was holding the *Gustloff* from pulling out? When—for God's sake—would they get the word to go? The questions were legion. A constant babel.

'Don't worry,' they'd answered at the start of it all. 'The Navy knows what it's about, and so does the Captain. Don't worry—it won't be long now, you'll see . . .'

But such reassurances had since worn so thin that they no longer even attemped to deploy them, but merely shrugged and tried to press on. Within yards, however, there would be yet another agitated swarm of questioners in their path.

In such circumstances even the simplest journey became a major operation, exacting a heavy toll on nerves and temper, and it wasn't long before the honeymoon between the sailors and the crowd was in danger of degenerating into a snarling match. Nor was the situation made any easier by the arrival of a party of VIPs in the small hours of the 30th. They were members of the family and personal staff of the port's Oberburgermeister and were accommodated—by order—in the ship's luxury suite, the Fuehrer-Kabin.

The contrast between the way in which these representatives of officialdom were housed—or were imagined to be housed—and the conditions that the ordinary refugees were obliged to suffer was far from passing unnoticed by the crowd. With the usual exaggeration, it was rumoured that the Burgermeister's party were living in style, and even had a separate boat reserved for them in case of accident! Try though they did to silence such highly embellished reports, the officers felt they were fighting a losing battle. In actual fact, far from their being entertained in solitary state, the members of the Burger-

meister's party were living in circumstances that were almost
as unpleasant as those surrounding the peasants, housed in the
decks below. The Fuehrer-Kabin was fine—for two people.
As things were, however, it was housing thirteen. The officers
weren't believed when they tried to explain the set-up. 'The
bigger the lie the more likely it is to be believed,' Herr Goebbels
had said. Ironically, as the 'Gustloffs' were now discovering, the
Reichminister had been very much on the mark.

It was not until dawn that anything even remotely resembling
tranquillity descended on the ship. Until then nobody, not even
the most exhausted, appeared to be able to sleep. Nor was the
current lull likely to last for long, the officers reflected. In such
conditions of stress and overcrowding the passengers were unlikely to indulge in more than a cat-nap, just sufficient to re-
fresh themselves for what doubtless would be a day of further
trials and tribulations.

Only in the crew's quarters was there anything approximat-
ing to the *Gustloff's* normal routine, and even here there were
notable divergencies. The off-duty watch were engaged in sleep-
ing or gambling, but there were less of them than was usual.
'Overtime' had proved obligatory in a ship with so many problems to take care of, and there were pointers even here to an
underlying unease. In one mess they chucked in a card game
in order to talk about the voyage, and speculate on their chances
*if,* it was argued, the voyage ever got started. For one thing
was sure, the men agreed—Base had better make its mind up
pretty smartly. If any more bodies were allowed to board the
ship pressure of numbers would burst her open at the seams!

Petersen, had they but known it, would have warmly second-
ed these apprehensive sentiments. Adding up the sum of his
responsibilities, he had just discovered that owing to the repeated delay in giving the ship a sailing time he was now in charge
of over 6,000 people : half as many again as the original 'over-
load'. If the *Gustloff* stayed put for much longer, she might
very well stay for ever.

It was 10 a.m. when Petersen finally received his long-awaited orders—10 a.m. on the 30th January, a day of bitter cold. Immediately he announced the glad news over the communication system, and then, taking advantage of the comparative calm that followed the initial excitement, he had the ship's regulations again read out to the crowd. Only by constant repetition could they be expected to make even the slightest impression on his variegated 'guests', and even so they would probably be very quickly forgotten. There were far too many distractions for passengers to focus on one issue at a time. However, one could but try.

Although the total number of those embarked was so greatly in excess of the original estimate, strenuous effort on the part of the ship's company had ensured that there were sufficient life-jackets to go round, and still leave some to spare. These were now distributed efficiently and smoothly, and with surprisingly few hitches, the passengers maintaining a good order that would have been inconceivable only a few hours before. However uncertain the hazards of the journey ahead it was quite clear that they held less terrors for the *Gustloff*'s new family than the prospect of a further stay in harbour. Everyone's spirits brightened at the thought of leaving this depressing scene behind them.

But not all of those who welcomed the news of the ship's imminent departure were destined in the end to travel in her. Men who had served in her throughout most of her Gotenhafen commission were among those who had to leave her, just as she had got the word to go. The decision for this disappointing sequel to the excitement of the morning was announced from Headquarters almost at a moment's notice, and took everyone by surprise.

It had been stated that Gotenhafen was to be defended 'to the last man' and would 'never surrender', but Base suddenly appeared to have a change of heart. 'Facilities' must be destroyed to avoid them falling into the hands of the port's besiegers. The *Gustloff* must provide a detachment to blow up the installations at Oxhöft. This unexpected addition to his multiple preoccupations gave Petersen the option of detailing men for the job or calling for volunteers. He chose to adopt the latter course. It was an unpleasant thing to have to do—to call on men to sacrifice their escape chances and adopt a role that could lead them only to captivity or death. And it was doubly unpleasant by reason of the fact that the *Willi G*'s 'family'— what remained of it—had been so close-knit by shared adversity. When Petersen made his appeal it was with a heavy heart, and he was deeply moved by his men's response.

The required force was raised in a matter of minutes—and raised without recourse to fanaticism or the 'Party Spirit'. The volunteers came forward quietly and without fuss : young men with serious faces, craftsmen considering the best way of doing their job. As they embarked, together with their explosives, in one of the *Gustloff*'s 'collapsibles' even the most cynical and case-hardened of the officers felt a brief glow of compassion and pride. God knows the ship had recently witnessed enough of selfishness at work. It was a change to see the other side of the picture. The young men cast off in sombre silence. A moment later the silence was broken by one of the girls of the Helferinnen, sobbing her heart out.

Shortly after the demolition party's departure yet another cause of delay arose. The promised escort for the ship could not be found, and it would be hours before she could be provided with a substitute. If she sailed at noon, as planned, the *Gustloff* would be entirely unprotected. It was the last straw. The final aggravation. A lesser man than Petersen might have yielded to despair. If he now persisted in sailing, the ship would be on her own. And not only the ship—but the six thousand lives aboard her. All would be reliant on the *Gustloff*'s luck. But if he didn't sail until he was given an escort, the ship might never get away from the jetty. Faced by this brutal dilemma, he chose to delay no further. 'We will sail as planned,' he told his assembled officers.


The *Wilhelm Gustloff* began her last voyage on the stroke of noon.

As she pulled away from the jetty a deep groan arose from the thousands—tens of thousands—who now stretched into the distance as far as the eye could see.

The ship's upper deck was thick with people—'like a stadium' it was said—who had poured from her interior to bid their farewell to the land, and as she cleared the naval harbour the hooters of other craft saluted her.

High up on the wings of the bridge, the duty signalman reported : '*Lutzow* making a signal, sir.' Their gaze switched to the lean and unprepossessing pocket battleship, and the message it was sending across the water.

'Very well, let's have it, then.'

'Gute Fahrt [Good cruise]' the signalman translated.

Petersen smiled and returned a courteous 'thank-you', then turned his attention to the Navigating Officer.

He was not to know the depth of feeling with which the Communications Officer had translated that signal—the last visual signal the *Gustloff* would ever receive.

To Petersen and the Captain of the *Lutzow,* 'old ships' though they were, the message was a simple act of courtesy. But to Lieutenant Fleischer it was very much more than that— a heartfelt wish for the safety of his bride.

CHAPTER FOUR

## *Kameradschaft*

INSIDE THE Gulf the going had been easy, although the wind
was freshening rapidly and it had started to snow. But now, as
the *Gustloff* edged her way out of the Roads and started to
round the lean fingertip of the Hela Peninsula, she began to get
a foretaste of the Baltic's violence, and found herself bucking
against a rising gale. Stumbling into the fug of the crew's quarters, men coming off watch reported that ice had frozen hard
on the rails and was sheathing the blocks in the davits on the
boat-deck. And it was getting even colder. A bloody awful
night.

Up on the command bridge—its thick glass windows dulling
the rising clamour of the wind and sea—Petersen could hear
the Navigating Officer and the Quartermaster recite their
litany, enhancing with their low-pitched exchanges the almost
cloistered calm that reigned there in contrast to the tumult outside.

'Steady on three-twelve, Sir . . .'

'Very well . . .'

The ship was now on course for the Stolpe Bank. With luck
she would be in Kiel by tomorrow teatime. After an almost
automatic glance at the dark mass of the Samland, on the far
side of the Gulf, Petersen rang the telegraph for Full Ahead.

Slowly the *Gustloff* began to gather speed, her tall sharp stem
tearing into the swell and transforming it into a huge inverted
V; a white-flecked creation which rose so high that its spray

44

rained down on the main deck and even speckled the wheel-house. Petersen permitted himself a smile of satisfaction. With her 27,000 tons of weight behind her, the *Gustloff* would be slowed only fractionally by the weather which in all other respects would be acting as her ally. For a submarine to be able to attack, let alone hit, the ship in these conditions would be a chance of rather more than a thousand to one.

'It's going to be an extra dirty night,' he said, almost gaily to the coterie around him.

'Dirty for Ivan,' retorted his Number One.

Insensibly, the atmosphere had relaxed. The tension that had gripped them all while the *Gustloff* was tied to the shore had lifted the moment she had first got under way. No longer was there any doubt about the Captain's decision to ignore the evasion plan. A zig-zag course would have been superfluous in this sort of sea.

The darkness, which had fallen early, was rapidly thickening; a darkness laced by the grey of driving sleet and tempered, far astern, by a vast red glow.

Out on the wings, the lookouts squinted at it through their night-glasses and then referred it to the Officer of the Watch, but it was too far away for them to trace it to its source. Approximately, it appeared to stem from somewhere behind Pillau, the port opposite Gotenhafen on the far side of Danzig Bay. Rosier than any summer sunset, though obscured at intervals by great gouts of snow, the glare broadened, narrowed, and broadened once again, as if at the whim of every gust of the ice-edged wind.

'The battle for Koenigsberg,' someone hazarded.

'It couldn't be . . . ' but his comrade didn't finish the sentence.

True that the front, supposedly, was over fifty miles away, but man-made infernoes these days threw their reflections far, and 'fronts' could move backwards fast in this area of mobile warfare. Even the local radio had admitted that this, the historic capital of the 'fortress' of East Prussia, had been enduring repeated assault. Against 'the hordes of Asia' it was 'resisting with a Will of Steel!'

And then, as the bridge personnel continued to ponder on the significance of the glow, the western sky began to lighten too. The Anglo-Saxons were paying their almost nightly visit to the Reich, but this time the target was far west of the Danzig area. Even the thunder of the flak was reduced to a whisper.

'Berlin, maybe?'

The speculation was met by a shrug: his audience maintaining a philosophic calm. At least it wasn't *their* turn to suffer, and for this they were duly thankful. Besides, there were other things for them to devote their minds to: the mine threat, for example.

On making his controversial decision to sail without an escort, Petersen had stressed that the ship would be in safe waters until dark, and that air cover would be provided from first light. Nor would the *Gustloff* be completely on her own in the (unlikely) event of a Russian surface raid during the night. For the first few hours of darkness the *Admiral Hipper* and her attendant destroyer would be within easy call, while there were E-boats and similar craft on tap in the peninsula. But in any case the prospects of surface attack were so slight as to be almost infinitesimal: what was far more to be feared was an encounter with a mine—'and whether it's "theirs" or "ours" won't matter very much. . . .' At the time there had been grim smiles of agreement from his audience: they all knew what the Captain had in mind.

The channels through the wide minefields defending the approaches to the Gulf were continually being swept, but there was always the danger of encountering a 'rogue'. Torn from their moorings by the buffeting of the weather, such breakaways were always a very real menace in these crowded waters and particularly so during the winter gales. Again, the long-range maritime aircraft of the Royal Air Force had become increasingly active. In recent weeks a vast quantity—literally thousands—of British mines had been dropped from the air to booby-trap the doors of the Baltic ports. Russian aircraft had also stepped up their quota, and were now operating from close range, from the airfields they had overrun in Lithuania. The mine threat to the *Gustloff* had to be taken very seriously, and Petersen had ordered the lookouts to be doubled.

In other respects, however, it was felt that the ship had very little to worry about. The chances of an attack by sea were remote, to say the least. By land and air the Russians had seized the initiative with a vengeance, but afloat it was a vastly different story. Despite the bravery of its crews the Red Fleet's performance had been uninspired and ineffective, and looked like remaining so. From the start of the war in the East, it had displayed an almost masterly inactivity. Even when the flanks of the Wehrmacht advancing on Leningrad had been wide open to assault from the sea, the Russians had made no attempt at intervention. Although the big ships of the German surface fleet had been committed to the Battle of the Atlantic, the eastern enemy had made little effort to venture out of the Gulf of Finland, but had stayed there until the weather locked him in. Even the Soviet Union's much-publicised submarine fleet, of which great things were expected, had failed to an extent that was almost total. Said to be as strong in numbers as the sea-wolves themselves, its few attempts at offensive action had revealed grave deficiencies in training and equipment. Its tactics were out-dated and its boats stayed near their bases.

Not until the summer of '44, when the German armies in the North had begun to crack beneath the hammer-blows of the mammoth Russian land offensive, had there been any significant sign that the Red Fleet might begin to pursue a more active role and seek to influence events outside its own home waters.

With the freeing of the German grip on the Kronstadt approaches and the subsequent capitulation of the Finns, its submarines had begun to launch isolated attacks on transports and supply ships in the north-eastern Baltic. Surface ships, though in small numbers, had attempted to bombard the by-passed German 'pockets' on the coastline. But overall, despite the Wehrmacht's catastrophic defeats on land, and the consequent fall of Riga and other Kriegsmarine bases, the Baltic was still very much a German lake.

'No, we've nothing to worry about, except the mines,' the watch reflected, 'and in this bloody murk a whole flock could go unnoticed. The weather's so thick.'

All the same, it was good to be at sea again. Ashore, they'd felt the old tub was a sitting duck for Ivan.

Relief that the *Gustloff* was at last in her natural element, and no longer subject to the vagaries of the shore establishment, was by no means confined to the ship's company and the bridge. Seasick though many of them were, it was shared to the full by the broad mass of her passengers—the anonymous folk who were crowded together in the decks below.

Even the peasant farmers from the Marches had become almost reconciled to their lot. Severed from the soil their families had worked for six centuries and more, people to whom the sea had hitherto been a mystery, and therefore endowed with menace, they had settled in their temporary refuge with resignation, and even gratitude. Jammed together cheek and jowl though they were, life was better—could not be worse!—than it had been during the nightmarish trek that had brought them here. Or so they thought.

Bombed and machine-gunned from the air, shelled by advanced patrols of the enemy's armour, hungry, sleepless, freezing yet stinking of sweat, the bulk of the refugees had come on foot—their children too. Even for those with transport—the lucky few who had managed to save their farm carts from 'requisition' by the hard-pressed soldiers—the long trek had

been unforgettable for its hardships. Presenting easy targets to
the far ranging fighter-bombers, their progress had been pain-
fully slow, while the wooden wheels of the carts, piled high with
their possessions, had made an impact almost as painful on the
bones as the icy roads had made on the walkers' feet. To people
like these, even the stench that their collective humanity had
caused to rise from the *Gustloff*'s bowels—'stinks like a sewer'
said an officer, briefly visiting—was a merely minor affliction.
In weeks, they had become inured to greater hardships than
their ancestors had experienced over the centuries. Respite was
precious.

It was from another, vastly different class of passenger from
the countryfolk that there came complaint and anger at the
ship's overcrowding. Perhaps predictably, it came from those
who were suffering the least : among them, the wives of the
two VIPs who had clashed with the guards on the gangplank.
Still smarting at that rebuff to their husbands, the women had
gone to the reception desk on B-deck to protest bitterly that
they'd been obliged to share 'their' cabin with three others, less
influential than they.

'They have no right to be there,' said one of the 'Party wives'
angrily. 'The place is furnished for two passengers only, and
we both have priority passes.'

'Madam,' the attendant answered, 'it's regrettable, but it's
purely due to the emergency.'

But they refused to be mollified.

'Utterly shameful,' said the senior of the pair. 'We had no
idea that things could be so bad. For people in our position to
be forced to share a pokey little cabin with three utter no-
bodies...'

It was then that, to the man's relief, an officer intervened.
Astounded at the attitude of the women—'unrealistic' was how
he later described it with masterly restraint—he, too, tried to
explain the situation's urgencies, only to meet with rebuff.

'The Navy should have told us what to expect before we

joined the ship,' the woman protested. 'We were brought here under what amounts to false pretences.'

'But surely you wouldn't have expected us to leave these people behind? You would not suggest we should abandon them to the Bolsheviks?'

It was an implication that would have frightened lesser folk, but the Party wife was undaunted. 'People like us are entitled to *some* comfort,' she stubbornly replied. 'The Town Commandant knows our husbands—men who have made sacrifices for the Reich. He would never have tolerated us being treated like this . . .'

The officer's comment was brief, and exceedingly vulgar.

'I'll report you,' the woman shouted. But he had turned his back, and left her.

As he gratefully sought refuge in the crowd, the Lieutenant was surprised to find himself shaking—shaking with rage. The incident, though seemingly so trivial, seemed suddenly to have epitomised the hopelessness of the Homeland's plight, and the futility of all attempts to put it right. The selfish sods! In conduct like theirs was the seed of the nation's ruin. However, as he realised a few moments later, not all of the *Wilhelm Gustloff*'s 'priority' passengers were so demanding as the pair from whom he had so rudely retreated. The girls of the Helferinnen, for example, were trying hard to make the best of things.


Settling down in their communal 'bed' in the drained-off swimming pool, and exchanging banter, predictably coarse, with the soldiers camping out on its tiled surround, the cheerfulness and adaptability of the 'helfs' warmed everyone.

Should anything really serious happen to the *Gustloff*, these girls would find it very hard to make the boat-deck, and they knew it. The pool was positioned seven decks down, and the way to the stairs would probably be jammed by people fleeing from the cabins and the engine-room. Yet they contrived to put a brave face on it all, as if the voyage was being made for fun.

Soon after the ship left harbour they had raised their voices in song. They cheered the Lieutenant, and temporarily lifted his gloom. They would have cheered even the wounded, had the wounded been able to hear them. But the wounded were housed elsewhere, in lazarets far-removed from each other, in widely separated areas of the ship. For some there were the cheerful wards on the promenade- and sun-decks: glass enclosed, and not far from the boats. But others had had to be berthed in far less agreeable quarters, well below, and for these the only sound was the rhythmic pounding of the *Gustloff*'s engines, and the thud of the sea against the hull.

Yet even this served more to reassure than alarm the helpless cot cases; those of them who were conscious enough to comprehend its meaning. They were even more isolated from escape than were the Helferinnen, yet there had been a general lightening of mood among them once the ship had parted with the shore. Even now, with seasickness adding to their general discomfort, those not under morphia or drugs were reasonably cheerful. The shore had held worse terrors for them than anything they might expect to encounter from the sea. Victims of frostbite and shock as well as bomb and bullet, the wounded had felt little confidence in the security offered by the *Gustloff* while the ship had been dallying in harbour. To many, the over-riding fear had been the enemy bombers, but others had felt there was danger of a change of heart at the High Command. Say the regime should lay down new criteria for evacuees? Say it should decide that the rescue of wounded was a luxury the Wehrmacht could not, at this stage, afford? While the *Gustloff* had remained in Gotenhafen, the speculations of the men in the wards had wandered far, and their conclusions had been unbelievably grim.

Most of them well-tried veterans with bitter experiences to draw on, they knew all too well how 'authority' could push a man around. 'Kits on, kits off' was not an exclusively Anglo-

Saxon routine, and they regarded all promises with cynical disbelief. Thus the pledges that the *Gustloff* would be used to carry them home had been received by them with a scepticism that was deep and fearful, disguise it though they did with their grouses and their jests. Only when the ship's screws had at last begun to turn had they dared to think that there might still be a future for them.

A man whose legs had been reduced to stumps produced an accordion and began to play it. Others joined in, accompanying the musician with their voices. There was suddenly a tremendous uplift in morale. They were getting out of the war, for a little while at least. They were on their way home, however changed 'home' might be. They were leaving behind them the East Front's unprecedented beastliness. Yet, even now, they could scarcely believe their luck.

The sea grew angrier, the glass fell, by 8 p.m. the *Gustloff* was driving through a miniature blizzard. At times, the bridge lookouts had their range of vision restricted to less than fifty yards. The snow swept in flurries against the square windows of the wheelhouse, and soon had settled along almost the entire length of the deck.

It was already three degrees colder than at the time of sailing, and the temperature was still falling. Crew members whose duties obliged them to venture into the open moved cautiously and crab-wise on planks that were already icing over. Up top on the boat-deck, the only sounds to intrude on the howl of the rising gale and the bluster of the sea were the creaks and groans of the davits, and the whiplike crack of the canvas topping the pile of floats that had been stacked below it in the stern.

Sent to make the fastenings secure, a working party found the going even bloodier than they'd thought. Fumbling with the wires and ropes that held the floats together, their hands were raw and frozen within seconds. Their breath was almost knocked from their lungs by the violence of the wind. Huge snowflakes filled their eyes and coated their lashes. When they staggered back gratefully into the fug below, they agreed that it was a sod of a night outside. Schnaps proved a great comforter.

On the bridge, however, where they were cushioned against the worst incivilities of the weather, there was small concern about such minor details as the transient discomforts of the ship's company or the scenic and sound effects of the Baltic's wildness; the *Gustloff* in her heyday had weathered far worse. They had the satisfaction of knowing that the ship was making good progress despite the prevailing conditions, and their calculations were that she would not be much overdue. With luck, said the Navigator, she would be arriving at Kiel by teatime : at the latest, they would be there in time for supper. As he spoke, they glanced involuntarily at the clock. It was 8.30 p.m. Eight hours had passed since the *Gustloff* had first got under way, and everything had proceeded strictly according to plan. The ship, though so long harbour-bound, was behaving magnificently : a thoroughbred in her natural element, however boisterous its welcome. There was no hint—no hint at all—of what was to come. The *Wilhelm Gustloff* was only forty-two minutes short of disaster.

## CHAPTER FIVE

# The Triple Blow

IN ONE of the few intervals he could spare from his otherwise all-absorbing preoccupation with the major business in hand—the safe progress of his ship—Petersen found time to wonder briefly how the passengers were finding it. It did not require a vast exercise of the imagination to conjecture that for many the answer would be 'pretty bad', and he felt a twinge of sympathy for their plight. What was rough for the ship's company would doubtless be hell for the landsmen, and even worse for the women and children. All the same, if they only knew it, they were lucky. Foul weather was better by far in wartime than a still, smooth sea : better because safer from the chance of attack. 'But try telling *that*,' said someone, 'to a man who is badly sea-sick!'

Seasickness was in fact the major affliction of the motley 6,000 who thronged the *Gustloff*'s overstrained living-space. Barred by the wildness of the night from ridding themselves of their nausea 'over the side', and served by toilets designed to cope with the needs of only a sixth of the ship's present mammoth population, their misery was acute and their example contagious.

Here and there were stalwarts who managed to surmount this pressing unpleasantness and even, in some cases, began to think of settling down for the night. Ruth Fleischer was one of this adaptable minority. To attempt to sleep seemed reasonable, she thought, for there was nothing else to do; nothing, that is, except to look back on the past, and *that* would have been almost unbearable : the contrast with the present was too acute. In one respect, however, she could count herself as being a shade more fortunate than her neighbours : if sleep she could, she had something soft to sleep on. Before the ship sailed, her husband had managed to wangle a mattress for her; an 'inflatable' of the new type, and hard to come by in a Germany where almost everything was dedicated to the needs of the war machine. An odd sort of gift from a newly-wed man to his bride? She had thought so at the time, and had laughingly said so, but now, she had to admit, there had been method in his madness. She had managed to find a corner in which there was a space to place her new possession, and had made a tolerable pillow of her coat. This done, her only discomfort—though this was major—was the heat. With the ports screwed tight the temperature in the big saloon was only a shade less oppressive than that which prevailed among the Balts—those of them who were housed in the decks below.

Shortly before the *Gustloff*'s departure, passengers had been warned that lifejackets must be worn throughout the voyage. In no circumstances were they to be removed, not even for short intervals. That some might ignore this specific order had probably never even occurred to Petersen, so rooted was he in the traditions of discipline and obedience. That some should choose to remove not only their lifejackets but part of their clothing as well, would have struck him as almost incredible. His charges surely should know that they must be prepared for any eventuality. Even lifeboat drill would be cruelly exacting in these icy conditions.

But for many of the evacuees the situation in the confined interior of the ship was such as to outweigh completely the arguments of sanity. The heat was intolerable, they complained, and lifejackets were discarded. Soon some of the men had stripped down to vests and trousers, while the women, discarding coats and jumpers, were wearing only their skirts and blouses. That Ruth did not support these acts of overt mutiny

was due, however, to a factor far removed from naval discipline, and arose from considerations that were almost entirely
sentimental.

'If anything should happen to the ship,' her husband had
warned, 'the worst enemy will be the cold. So promise me you'll
wear your warmest things—and keep them on.'

'What if I have to swim for it?' she'd teased.

'You'll have your lifejacket to support you,' he had answered,
heavily serious. 'The cold can kill you far faster than the sea.'

Again she had laughed, though not without a heartache at
this manifestation of his concern for her. 'Don't worry about
me,' she said. 'The Navy will take care of *me*. It's I who should
be worrying about you.'

But he had still insisted : 'Promise me . . .'

And so, she'd promised. . . .

There had been tears between them as they had said their
goodbyes. There were tears on their way as she thought about
him now. Five days of honeymoon ended on the crowded quayside . . . and now this, the unknown. Embarrassed, she had to
close her eyes so as not to show her softness to this roomful of
strangers.

'You're all muffled up, Fraulein,' said one of the shirt-sleeves
brigade, good-naturedly enough. 'Why don't you shed your
coat? You must be boiling.'

She shook her head.

Yes, it was hot all right, but somehow or other she must learn
to bear it. She must sweat it out, in the literal sense of the word.
To have done otherwise would have been an act of gross
betrayal.


For sixteen-year-old Ilse Bauer were far less tender memories
of the shore than those that haunted the bride of five days,
Frau Fleischer. Not for Ilse was the softness of young love, but
an anguish that turned her slumbers into nightmares,

When word had come to her parents to evacuate their small farm in East Prussia they had decided to obey, but not to panic. Unlike their neighbours, who had fled with no more than a suitcase or two to show for their long years of toil, the Bauers were determined to be prudent, and had proceeded with their packing at a steady methodical pace. They were still several miles behind the front—or so they thought—and hard-headed Papa Bauer wanted to salvage all he could. He had not slaved for a lifetime only to leave his next of kin without a schilling.

The wagon had been loaded, the horses harnessed, and the Bauers were about to leave when the soldiers came. . . .

A score of squat unshaven men in fur caps with large ear-flaps—Mongolians or Tartars, perhaps, but it did not really matter—they swooped on the farm with total unexpectedness, as astonishing in their appearance as visitors from another planet, a savage planet.

Part of a detachment from the advance guard of Rokossov-sky's army, somehow they had filtered through the wide-spaced ranks of the defenders and now, two days later, were on the rampage, and hopelessly out of hand. They grabbed Papa Bauer and stood him in front of the tailboard of his cart and then, while Ilse watched, they shot him dead. When Frau Bauer threw herself upon his body they hauled her up by her hair and shot her too. And after that they turned on Ilse.

It was twenty-four hours before the invaders departed, their line of retreat being threatened by a local panzer counter-attack. They left Ilse living, but unconscious and bleeding, spreadeagled and naked on the straw of the barn floor.

When, guided by a neighbour, a German patrol reached the farm, it was to find the girl in convulsions of agony and terror. She screamed at the sight of them, and continued screaming—but perhaps 'screaming' was not the word. The sound came up from her throat like a demented croak. With the grim uncon-cern of men who had seen it all before, the soldiers brought her

to a field ambulance, burned down the Bauer farmhouse to
deny it to the enemy when he returned in force, and prepared
to rejoin their unit, soon to be in retreat again.

The process that had introduced Ilse to the *Gustloff* had taken
six months to complete, but she looked back on most of that
time as if through a haze, recalling, perhaps mercifully, very
little of its details. Only the general outline of her wanderings
remained imprinted on her brain, but the memory of the rape
that had preceded them would never be erased. The hairy
hands tearing off her skirt and underclothes . . . the brutal grip
of the man's companions, dragging her legs apart . . . the pant-
ing breath of her attackers . . . never could she hope to eradicate
the horrors of her ordeal.

Moved back from the battle area and transferred to civilian
care, she had subsequently been sent to hospital for treatment,
released as cured, and then, 'relapsed', had found herself in
hospital once more. It was there that—her body mended, but
her mind still sick—she had met her present companions,
suffering as much as she. All of them sexual casualties of the
current offensive, they had been sent to Gotenhafen just ahead
of the new Russian thrust.

Originally it had been intended to house them in the ship's
hospital, but this had proved to be completely out of the question : the hospital was overflowing with the Wehrmacht's
wounded. Service doctors, busy with burn, frostbite and ampu-
tation cases, had no time to attend to such low-priority afflic-
tions as the consequences of rape. Nor was there space available
in the ward off the sun-deck reserved for 'women only'. Mostly
this was earmarked for the pregnant; at least six of the patients
had reached their time.

However, Miss Bauer and four others of her group were
fortunate insofar as their condition aroused sufficient concern
on the bridge for them to be allotted a cabin instead of being

left to fend for themselves in the crowd. And for this concession
they were almost childishly appreciative. As Ilse was to explain,
many years later : 'We were sick of the sight of men, and
frightened of them too. We were disgusted with ourselves, and
with the past that hadn't been of our making. We were fed up
with the war, the crowds, and the ugliness of it all. We just
wanted to creep into a corner and hide ourselves. We just
wanted a little peace.'

They did not get it.


Climbing into the narrow bunk that was to be her temporary
'home' down on E-deck, Sigrid Bergfeld could also regard herself as 'privileged'—privileged in the sense that space had been
found for her in a cabin. But in her case the concession had been
made for the simple reason that there was nowhere else where
they could conveniently put her.

A Marine 'helf', seventeen-year-old Sigrid would normally
have been billeted with the rest of her comrades, but the pool
was already overcrowded when she and her section arrived
and it looked as though they would have to move to another
deck. In the military sense, however, such an arrangement
seemed untidy : helf officers liked to keep their troops together !
So in the end authority reached a compromise, by handing over
a cabin within shouting-range of the pool.

The accommodation thus provided was scarcely lavish.
Shared between Sigrid and five other girls, it allowed each of
them a living space of less than six feet by three. It was near to
the engine-room, and unbelievably stuffy. And yet, contrarily,
not one of them would have swapped places with the rest of
the crowd. It was good to feel independent . . . good to be
out of range of their leader's inquisitive eye . . . and as they
prepared to turn in for the night they congratulated themselves on their freedom, and the move that had made it
possible.

For Sigrid, however, it was to mean far more than that. The switch to the cabin had saved her life.

'U-boat warning. U-boat warning. Russian submarines reported on the northern route off the Stolpe Bank...'

The signal, sent out by GruppeOst, was picked up by the *Hipper*, then only a few miles west of the *Gustloff*, and accompanied by the escort destroyer *TZ 36*. The *TZ 36* also logged its receipt, as did most other units of the scattered fleet that was now travelling through the dark en route for Kiel and Flensburg. But even when the signal was repeated the largest ship of the lot, the *Wilhelm Gustloff*, did not hear it. For some reason or other, maybe freak weather conditions, the *Gustloff* was the exception to the rule. She never received the warning of the threat that lay in her path and, in ignorance, blundered on.

At 2100 hours the ship was maintaining her steady course and Petersen, indulging in one of his periodic reviews of the situation aboard her, was well satisfied with the way in which things appeared to be shaping. Considering what they had had to suffer, and were continuing to suffer, as a result of this really nasty switchback of a sea, the passengers, though miserable, were surprisingly well-behaved. To cope with their needs the commissariat staff had worked wonders by way of organisation, handicapped though they were, and this had paid off in terms of the ship's good order. All in all, there seemed small cause for concern and much for congratulation.

In the wards, the surgeon reported little sign of apprehension among the wounded, and even the fears of the peasants had died down. Doubts as to the efficiency of the ship's engines had proved unfounded, and the *Gustloff* was riding the weather even better than before.

It was twelve minutes later when the first torpedo struck.

It had been the good fortune of young Ivan Marinesko, commanding the Red Fleet submarine *S 13*, to sight the *Gustloff*—travelling fast, but at close range, and on a course that would bring her right in line with his bow torpedo tubes. The thousand-to-one chance had come off, and Marinesko and his crew could hardly credit it.

Despite the massive concentration of traffic in the sea approaches to the Gulf and the north-east pockets, the Russians' sole big catch to date had been the ancient pre-dreadnought battleship *Schleswig Holstein,* deemed too old for front-line service even in the Kaiser's war. Their bombers had sunk her in Danzig Bay. Even now, with the Red submarines at last out in force and seeking offensive action, expectations of the Navy bettering this unmemorable performance had not been high.

Ordered to patrol off the shipping lanes to the north of the Stolpe Bank and attack anything he might encounter there, Marinesko, on the face of it, had little chance of achieving any sensational success. If the weather could be said to be bad for the transports, it was appalling for a surfaced submarine. Yet to submerge and lie in wait at periscope depth would be to defeat the main purpose of his mission. Visibility being what it was, the *S 13* would be working blindfold.

In her build and performance, Marinesko's command was fairly typical of the new-generation Russian submarine. Of medium size, with a displacement of 760 tons, she had the relatively fast surface speed of 20 knots, dropping to 8·5 knots when submerged. One of a class of twelve laid down in the immediate pre-war period to give a new bite to what was otherwise an extremely aged fleet, she was robust and manoeuverable but lacked the technical refinements of her British and German opposite numbers, and this was particularly so in the field of direction-finding.

Thus, when he saw the *Gustloff* emerge from the murk ahead of him, Marinesko's elation almost took second place to his astonishment. Not one of the many small coasters used to supply the Wehrmacht along the beleaguered beaches . . . not even a landing-ship laden with tanks and guns . . . but the towering steep silhouette of an ocean liner, big enough to be carrying a regiment or more . . . here indeed was a worthy target!

For a moment he continued to stare at the fast approaching stranger, but whatever his feelings he did not dwell upon them for long. Instead, he turned to the men at the tubes and said evenly: 'Fire one . . . Fire two . . . Fire three.'


The first torpedo crunched into the *Gustloff*'s bows hurling everyone off their feet, and was followed very rapidly by the second, which exploded amidships. And then, as the klaxons clamoured, came the third and mortal blow, a torpedo that hit the engine-room.

A great hole was torn into the tall hull of the *Wilhelm Gustloff*. Hundreds of tons of salt water were unleashed on to the red-hot boilers. The men of the black gang were swept aside like straws, many of them being flayed alive by the boiling steam.

'We're done for!' someone screamed.

And then the lights went out.

## CHAPTER SIX

## Death in the Night

THE SECOND torpedo had hit the swimming pool housing the Helferinnen. The lucky ones died in their sleep; for others on the fringes of the pool fate was less kind. For seconds after the impact there was silence throughout F-deck. Bedlam followed.

Some of the girls were screaming from sheer shock, but dominating their screams was an animal cry of agony. Impossible to withhold, it rose from the throats of the handful who lived, as if dragged from them. A survivor was later to say : 'It chilled the blood.'

An A.B. came staggering towards the scene with a vague idea of helping. The emergency lighting had gone on, but he found it very difficult to see. Dust, displaced by the blast, was swirling across the companionway, and there was smoke as well; almost a fog. And then he encountered a wall where a wall should not have been, a wall made of debris, and his toecap stubbed into something soft and yielding, and he stumbled and fell.

'Sorry, Fraulein,' he said with idiot politeness to the girl who lay there, but she did not answer. Somehow she had managed to climb out of the abattoir that had claimed so many of her comrades, but after that she had collapsed, all effort spent.

'Let's get you on your feet,' he said, until, stooping to lift her, he saw her face. One side of it had the peach-like innocence of a pretty child. The other was a mask of skinless flesh and writhing sinew, like a skinned rabbit. The A.B. spewed.

Other would-be rescuers, choking from the dust and fumes

given out by the explosion, struggled towards the scene, only to recoil from the horrors that barred their way.

The big-bosomed, broad-bottomed, naked nymphs of the gaily painted mural—'classical Greek'—that had formerly dominated the pool had now collapsed across a sacrificial mound of shattered limbs and twisted bodies. In macabre parody of its former purpose, the smooth-tiled waste channel was running with blood.

'Let's go,' said someone. 'There's no work for us here . . .'


For Ilse Bauer, the passage of the torpedo, carving through the cabins on the starboard side of the ship before exploding, expressed itself as a tremendous blast of air. It threw her from her bunk and upended her, hurling her into the corner opposite. And then, abruptly withdrawing, it sucked the breath from her lungs, leaving her choking.

'Gases,' they later hazarded, gases thrown out by the missiles as they registered. At the time she was aware of no such fine definition, she felt she was being strangled. Even when she was able to breathe again and the roaring in her ears had subsided, she was utterly in the dark as to what had happened. Her head was aching, her cheekbones numbed. Completely confused, she couldn't—just couldn't—even begin to understand.

At one stroke the cabin had been transformed into a ruin, and had lost all resemblance to its former shape and purpose. As the emergency lights flickered on, she found herself looking up, in a sort of twilight, at a scene to which only a surrealist could have attempted to do justice. A sort of crazy jungle, in which all shapes and sizes were represented and seemingly interlocked. Great strips of metal with curling, jagged edges . . . a heap of upturned mattresses, part degutted . . . a *chevaux de frise* of fractured timber . . . she couldn't make any sense of her surroundings. It would cost her an effort to focus and find a meaning for it all : and somehow she did not want to, perhaps because the meaning would hurt. Only when her hand connected unexpectedly with the body that lay beside her, clammy and unresisting to her disorientated touch, did Ilse's dulled brain clear. *This* was the body of one of her cabin-mates, and across it had fallen two more. She was alone with the dead.

To this day, Ilse cannot remember exactly what happened next : the affair was traumatic. But, with her reflexes triggered off by terror, she must somehow have pushed aside the debris that blocked the hole where the door had been and managed to crawl through it. In the corridor she found herself in the midst of a human sea.

After the stresses imposed by their previous experiences, the *Gustloff*'s passengers had been in no shape to react calmly to the torpedo attack. Fear spread among them like an epidemic. Neither were they in the mood to respond to the pleas for order that were being made over the ship's internal broadcasting system. In fact very few of the hundreds crammed together on F-deck even heard them. The system itself had broken down beneath the force of the explosions, some later claimed, but others placed the blame on the din created by their fellow victims, a din so loud, they said, that nothing could be heard above it.

Groups drawn from the ship's company had earlier been detailed to help control the passengers in the event of emergency, but when the event materialised nothing was seen of them. Except for a few isolated individuals—Canutes against the tide—the control teams might never have exsisted for all that they did by way of intervention. It was subsequently argued that their non-appearance was due to the sheer volume of the crowd; its mass had been so thick that they had been unable to penetrate. But Ilse, for one, was unaware that they were trying. There was no evidence that she could see of leadership or planning. Pressed so tightly by those around her that she had no power to move except by the volition of the mob, she was like all others—at the mercy of its whims. She was swept

c

with it on its course as helplessly as a cork upon a wave-top. It was when it reached the stairs that led to the deck above that the 'tide' transformed itself into a destructive whirlpool, dragging its victims down beneath its agitated surface. The tough fought their way up the steps, and gave no mercy. The weak were trampled underneath their feet.


In the cabin where she had been housed with her comrades of the Helferinnen for whom there had been no room in the pool, Sigrid Bergfeld's awakening was prefaced by the blast of the explosion and accompanied by a sense of terror so acute that she bit her tongue.

She was in complete darkness and unable to move. Her legs had a great weight pressing down on them, and were gripped as if by a vice. There was a deafening noise in her ears, though she could not identify it. When the emergency lights went on she found that from the knees downward her limbs were hidden by a mound of tumbled furniture, and that the noise was the roar of water. It was cascading through a yawning hole in the bulkhead, and rapidly climbing.

For long seconds she stared at the scene as if in a trance, incapable of uttering a sound. And then she became aware that Irma, her friend, was beside her, clawing at the wreckage to try and set her free, and crying as she did so. Tears accompanied every effort.

'For God's sake, tell me what's happened!' screamed Sigrid, returning to life. 'And where are the others?'

'I think they're dead,' sobbed her cabin-mate.

Weakly, the 'helf' still helped by the other girl struggled out of the trap, and got slowly to her feet. The water was already ankle-deep, and increasing its rate of climb.

'We'll be drowned if we stay here,' she said.

'Then let's get out!'

But when they tried the door they discovered it would not

budge. It had been jammed shut by the force of the explosion, and they tugged at it in vain.

Momentarily, they were so shocked by this reverse that they almost gave up. It seemed impossible that they could take any more. But then they noticed that a crack had opened on the inward side of the cabin, and they plunged through the tide to get at it and make it wider. They were up to their waists in water before the crack was big enough for them to pass through, and they were able to emerge into the companionway almost next door to the engine-room. But even then their chances seemed very slim.

Men of the black gang in flight from the scalding steam . . . walking wounded from the lazaret's 'extension' . . . low-priority civilians shipped almost as an afterthought—like the displaced occupants of an upturned hive they swarmed in their hundreds across the escape lane, stinging and overwhelming all who got in their way. At this level the main staircase had been blocked by debris. The emergency stairs were now the sole surviving link with the rest of the ship, and the crowd made for them with frightening ruthlessness.

Parted from her friend by the blind fury of the onrush, pushed, jostled and squeezed by the mass of people around her, Sigrid could do nothing—nothing at all—except allow herself to be swept along on the prevailing current. The crush was so thick that she could not move her arms. They were pinioned to her body by the sheer weight of her neighbours. She could not move even her feet. She was carried forward, unresisting, as if on air.

At one stage of the journey, of which she was barely conscious, the crowd's passage was interrupted by some unknown obstacle and she almost fell. But sheer terror, and someone's arm, yanked her back to her feet again. It was an escape that, as she later realised, was almost miraculous. To fall was usually fatal. Once down, a fugitive was seldom allowed to rise again.

Perhaps when they managed to reach the next deck things

would be easier? It was a thought that helped support the few who still could think amid this chaotic flight from the stricken area. But when they got to E-deck it was to have their frail hope falsified. If anything, the carnage at the top of the stairs was worse than the carnage below.


Still helplessly a prisoner of the crowd, Ilse Bauer felt herself stumbling on a floor that was mattress-soft, and yet uneven. A floor composed of the bodies of those who had fallen beneath the unseeing throng's stampede. At one point, where the corridors converged on the stairs, the dead were lying in tiers— 'like sandwiches' she was later to recall. But still the mob did not change its course. It was not that nobody cared. Even when their terror was at its peak those nearest a person falling would instinctively try to hold back. But they were powerless to withstand the weight of the mass behind them, propelled in turn by pressures still further to the rear. Very few of those who fell ever got to their feet again. Women, children and invalids—the crowd's panic was indiscriminate in its choice of victims.

Between the fugitives and their goal—the fancied security afforded by the lifeboats—lay seven deck levels, the entrance to each of them becoming a narrow bottleneck and creating hazards that grew greater every moment, as each deck contributed its quota to the human tide. In such circumstances slightest obstacle to the progress of the crowd served to add to the grim toll that it had already exacted. A door that did not immediately open to the touch cost the lives of twenty, crushed against it. An unseen step, by tripping one man, caused the deaths of several more who fell on top of him. The rest of the people trod them down. When they eventually reached the entrance to the maindeck, Ilse was shot into the open like a bullet from a gun.

Ruth Fleischer, her cat-nap shattered, awoke to find that the big saloon was on the move. Cases, haversacks, blanket-rolls and bundles were sliding across the slanting floor, as if animated by a motive power that came from within themselves rather than from the giant's punch that had set the *Gustloff* swaying. Momentarily she was overcome by the sheer surprise of it all, but then someone screamed, and she roused herself to action.

Alarm bells were hammering through the length of the ship. She heard a voice over the tannoy say something about mustering at the boat stations, and there followed a reminder to passengers not to forget to bring their lifejackets. From the transmission system crackled a further string of commands and reassurances, but the words were so garbled that she could not understand them properly. She just looked at the course the rest of the crowd was taking, and followed suit.

It was only when they emerged into the open that they realised just how thoroughly they had been cocooned against the weather. Once they had passed through the huge plate-glass doors that opened from the sun-deck their breath was almost plucked from their lungs by the force of the wind. It sent its sharp fingers through even the thickest clothing. It drove the snow horizontally into their faces. They were chilled to the bone. The surface of the deck had iced over, sending them slipping and sliding down its steepening slope towards the guard-rails. Minutes passed before Ruth could take stock of her surroundings. Only faintly discernible in the dim glow of the emergency lamps, a handful of seamen were already at work on the lifeboats. The davits were sheathed in ice, and axes and hammers had to be employed to free them. Other men were clustered around the floats. From the top of the funnel, towering above them in the dark, came a continuous spray of noisy steam. As yet, however, the fugitives in Ruth's vicinity were far from experiencing the total despair that had overwhelmed the multitudes on the lower decks. Comparatively few in numbers, they were so far uncontaminated by the panic that had accounted

for so many lives in the deep interior of the ship, and were in
general quite well-behaved and amenable to orders.

Queues began to form at the boat station, and the traditional
priorities were being meticulously observed. With the men standing back, and the women and children passing through them
to the front, the deck presented a picture of discipline and sanity
that was, unfortunately, too good to last. It ended with a fresh
influx of refugees from below, an onrush of people out of their
minds with fright.


Scarcely had the first lifeboat been freed than there was a
frenzied stampede towards it.

'Women and children first!' an officer yelled, but the newcomers were too shocked by their recent experiences to pay any
heed. In a matter of seconds they had shattered the nearest of
the queues, absorbing its fragments into their own hysterical
mass. Punching, kicking, oblivious to all standards but those
created by their fears, they swarmed over the boat, and as they
did so, people who had hitherto been content to observe discipline broke from their stations to oppose them. From a brave
attempt at orderly evacuation, the situation had been transformed into a free-for-all, a battle for individual survival in
which victory went to the strong.

A woman had her baby dashed from her arms by one of the
queue-jumpers. A small boy, crushed against the guard-rail
by the mob, slipped—no one knew how—and fell into the sea.
And then, as the ropes began to slide from the davits, and the
boat began its descent, a score or more from the crowd jumped
after it, landing on top of its terrified occupants.

Given the confusion of the launching, and the fact that the
craft was already carrying far more than its authorised maximum load, the result was inevitable. The lifeboat hit the water
at speed, bounced violently and capsized. A mass of struggling
bodies, thrown from it like so many pieces of confetti, danced

briefly on the froth that burgeoned from the point of impact. And then the victims had dispersed and vanished, obliterated by the embrace of a gigantic wave.

The crowd sobered up.

If the scene on the boat-deck had got temporarily out of hand, it was small stuff indeed compared with the chaos that was raging in the interior of the ship. On the bridge, however, they were as yet unaware of the toll being exacted in the crowded companionways, rapidly flooding, and were still confident that they would be able to maintain discipline, if little else.

Determinedly a professional, Petersen had been quick to recover from the initial shock of the disaster, and equally quick to react against it. So his gamble had failed, and failed absolutely! Through the oddest of odd chances—no planning could have arranged it in this frightful weather—a submarine had been lying directly in the *Gustloff*'s path, and now he was left to bear the ghastly consequences. 'A chance in a million', one of his officers described it, but Petersen knew that it was hopeless to cry 'accident'. His career was threatened with a ruin as total as that which would overwhelm his ship. He had had damnable bad luck, but he *had* made an error of judgement. Yet it was on the *Gustloff*, not on his future, that Petersen kept his attention focused in this period of confusion. The *Gustloff* and the 6,000 in his charge. Outwardly still very much in command of the situation he presented an appearance of confidence and calm. A pity, they said later, that it failed to make much impact beyond the bridge.

The Captain's first move was to order detachments of sailors to secure the boats, restore order among the crowd around them, and ensure that the women and children got priority in escape. Next, he ordered another detachment to guard the exits from the promenade-deck and sun-deck. At all costs there must be no further panicky rushes. The crowd below must be contained in both those areas, and 'siphoned through' to the boat stations in small groups, under supervision.

While he gave these decisive-sounding directives, Petersen was acutely aware of their limitations. From the preliminary damage reports, necessarily scant as they were, he had concluded that the ship, though wounded mortally, might live long enough for the boats to be got away. But even so the cost in life would be appalling. Barring the swift arrival of rescue craft, there could be no hope—no hope at all!—for well over half of the ship's unfortunate passengers. There just were not the boats available. The strictest discipline, the most meticulous good behaviour, would not be able to counteract the effect of the dreadful equation he had worked out when back in harbour. There was only one place available in the lifeboats for every five persons now on the ship. Nor could discipline alone sustain for long the multitudes who, with the temperature well below freezing, would have no recourse but the floats. And yet, without discipline, the tragedy would be even more calamitous in its effect. In a general save-who-can the weakest would go to the wall, and the boats would be overrun.

'If need be you must use iron measures to keep order,' he told his officers. They could crack down as hard as they liked on dissidents and troublemakers.

Only when he began to receive eye-witness reports of the situation from members of the ship's company who had experienced at close range the extent of the crowd's panic, did Petersen begin to have serious doubts as to the efficiency of his attempt to establish control. The *cordon sanitaire* he had aimed to erect between the boats and the broad mass of the fugitives from below decks was late in forming, and those comprising it were likely to be too few.

'Have we had any answer to our signals?' he asked.

'Not yet, sir,' came the reply.

Had Petersen been able to see the state of the W/T room he would quickly have realised why.

## CHAPTER SEVEN

# A Cry from the Dark

AT 9 p.m. the duty operators presiding over the gleaming bank of W/T sets that stretched along the bulkhead of the *Gustloff*'s communications-room, were finding that time lay heavy on their hands. They were relaxed and comfortable, but more than a trifle bored. Traffic had been so light as to be almost non-existent. The ship was maintaining the wireless silence that had been ordered on her departure from the Gulf, and the other craft engaged in the evacuation were similarly still. There was little to be heard but Danzig Radio, and little for the men to do but listen to it, however sombre the deductions they might draw from what it said, or left unsaid, about the struggle reigning ashore.

At one stage women and children had been earnestly exhorted to do their share and clear the snow off the main roads leading west. At another, came a panegyric on the Volkssturm, 'swarming' from their homes and factories to 'hold back the Bolshevik hordes'. At each of these appeals for greater effort —pitched on ever more strident notes of urgency—the W/T men had exchanged significant glances, but few words had been spoken. They just did not want to talk about the meaning concealed by the flamboyant slogans, the mounting defeat and desperation among those that the *Gustloff* had left behind.

But now and then there had been breaks in reception, and that is perhaps why they never heard the warning. Static? The weather? No one was later to account for it in satisfactory style, but they missed completely the signal that was to presage their ship's destruction.

'Achtung! Achtung! Hostile submarines in sea area north of the Hela Peninsula . . .'

Well-seasoned though they were, and untroubled by heavy traffic, the *Gustloff*'s W/T staff never heard a word of it. By 9.15 Danzig's clarion calls to battle had died down, to be replaced by light orchestral music : harmless, sugary, in the Grand Hotel tradition, evocative of an era of potted palms and creamy teacakes. In the warmth of the communications-room, the men at the sets almost unconsciously relaxed.

It was the arrival of the torpedoes that brought the music, and the routine, to a total stop. When the dazed men recovered their wits it was to find the room filled with a blinding storm of dust. And then, when this subsided, thin wisps of smoke began to rise from the sets.

'The radio valves!' exclaimed the senior operator.

After a quick checkup it was evident that the transmitters were unworkable. Their valves had been shattered by the force of the blast. An emergency set was rigged up in only a matter of minutes, but every minute was precious, and the transmission was weak.

'SOS WILHELM GUSTLOFF, hit by three torpedoes . . . 6,000 people aboard . . .'

With the rest of the ship in chaos, the W/T men stayed at their posts and continued to transmit, but no answer was returned to the repeated signal. The air was still. Hadn't anyone heard them?


In the stuffy confinement of the tiny W/T cabin of the trawler-type minesweeper *M 341*, the one and only operator on duty heard the thin crackle of morse with a sense of irritation. It was weak stuff, and intermittent, and it was interfering with the music. But then, as he readjusted the earphones that, for com-

fort, he had pushed back around his neck, he recognised the
distinctive pattern of the opening; S.O.S. He reached for a
signal pad.

'SOS W . . . E . M G . . TLOFF, hit by three torpedoes . . .'

The message was imperfect, coming over in bits and pieces,
but as he spoke through the voice-pipe to the bridge he was
aware of a mounting apprehension.

'6,000 people aboard . . .'

He was stunned at what he had copied on to the pad. His
first thought was that he had made a crazy mistake. Six thousand! The figure was monumental. No single ship could carry
such a load of passengers. But then, on a repeat, he filled in the
gaps between the letters. The *Wilhelm Gustloff*. The big liner.

The Skipper called him. 'You did say the *Wilhelm Gustloff*?'

'I'm sure that it's her, sir . . .'

A moment later, a further repetition confirmed his hunch.

'What's her position?'

'She's not coming through very clear, sir.'

'Verdammt! But keep at it . . .'

More agonising minutes passed before they were able to
piece the whole of the message together and be positive about
it. The *Gustloff* must be quite close, perhaps twenty miles away.
But with the heavy sea, and *341*'s limited speed, it would take
the minesweeper at least two hours to close her. At the same
time, they reasoned, there was surely hope for the ship and her
myriad passengers. She was less than thirteen miles from the
shore and there were other ships in her vicinity, some of them
quite large. To these, and to Naval HQ, the *M 341* began to
retransmit the S.O.S. Pride of place among those who received
it went to a heavy cruiser, the well-known *Admiral Hipper*.


Measured by any standard, the *Admiral Hipper*'s wartime
career had been to date a fairly hectic one. It had also had its
quota of ups and downs, despite the nickname that her crew

had given her, of Das Glüchliche Schiff, or The Lucky Ship.

In her first sea-action, fought off Norway in 1940, the *Hipper*'s big eight-inch guns had claimed the British destroyer *Glowworm* as their victim. But even this 'success', against a ship less than one eighth of her size and with less than a twentieth of her weight in gunpower, had had its debit side for the cruiser. Although in her death throes, the *Glowworm,* having narrowly missed with torpedoes, had steamed at speed towards her mighty adversary and had rammed her, carving deep into her hull. After fire had ceased, and the two ships pulled apart, only thirty-eight of the destroyer's gallant company had survived to struggle up the scrambling nets lowered over the cruiser's side, but the *Hipper*'s damage squad were already finding that the 'victory' was hollow. With a twenty-five-foot hole gaping above her water-line, the ship was forced to break off her cruise and return to Bergen for repairs.

Nor was this the only time that the *Hipper*'s legendary luck had failed her when in confrontation with the British. Just two years after the *Glowworm* had nipped in the bud what had promised to be a long and successful foray, an operation with a similarly hopeful start had ended in reverse, this time as the consequence of a well-placed British shell. Flying the flag of Admiral Kummetz, and accompanied by the pocket battle-ship *Lutzow* and a powerful destroyer group, the *Hipper* had been part of a task force designed to annihilate the convoy *PQ 15* laden with vital war materials for Russia. Despite the vigilance of R.A.F. and R.N. patrols, the German squadron had succeeded in leaving harbour undetected and had reached the fringe of the convoy before being sighted, and attacked, by a pair of British destroyers.

It was a gallant action in the best *Glowworm* tradition, though it seemed at first to have been fought in vain. The destroyer *Achates* was sunk and her companion repulsed. The merchantmen were outpaced, and the Germans were soon clos-ing in for the kill. But then, unexpectedly, they found themselves engaged by the cruisers *Kent* and *Jamaica,* emerging suddenly from the murk and immediately opening fire.

On the face of it, this intervention presented little threat to Kummetz's objective. Each of the *Lutzow's* 11"-guns could throw treble the weight of metal disposed by the *Kent's* ageing 8", while the *Hipper's* own 8"-guns (a later model) were more than a match for the 6" (100 lbs) projectiles of *Jamaica.* Yet the British, although so heavily outclassed in the purely logistical sense, made up for the deficiency by their spirit and skill. Making the fullest use of the prevailing snow squalls, until then an asset to the Germans in masking their approach on the convoy, they had managed to take their enemies by surprise, and brought their fire to bear at relatively close range. The *Hipper* sustained a hit from their second salvo. The shell registered at a particularly critical moment, just as the ship was heeling over towards her adversaries. It ripped through the armoured deck, exploded in the engine-room, and almost immediately the cruiser began to lose way. Minutes later, Kummetz reluctantly decided to break off action and return to base.

It was a startling decision, and one that was to cost him dear. It was also to have momentous consequences, both on the conduct of the naval war in the West and the future of the German surface fleet. Haunted by Hitler's specific orders to 'take no unnecessary risks'—an order that had been repeated in a signal delivered to him at the very opening of the fight—the Admiral had felt that the laming of the *Hipper,* his most powerful ship, had left him no alternative but retreat. But this strict adherence to orders brought him no thanks from his superiors ashore. Having anticipated a spectacular victory, the Fuehrer's disappointment was intense—and so was his fury. The Navy was denounced for its 'lack of offensive spirit', and the very existence of the heavies was threatened.

It was not until she and the other maligned big ships had narrowly escaped a Hitler decree to 'scrap the lot', and had been relegated to the Baltic, that the *Admiral Hipper* had really be-

gun to live up to her 'lucky' legend. In a series of ship-to-shore
bombardments, unique in their pattern and extent, she and the
rest of the German heavy cruisers—the *Scheer, Lutzow* and
*Prinz Eugen*—had played a decisive part in the evacuation of
by-passed Army pockets in the Baltic States, and were soon to
be hammering at the Russian armour as it advanced into the
heart of the Homeland itself.

Currently, however, the ship was coping with a vastly different role, a role with which she was completely unfamiliar, and
her Captain was not taking too kindly to the change. It presented him with problems he would gladly have done without.
With her formidable armament and massive armour, her fast
speed and long-range endurance, the cruiser had been tailored
for offensive forays against the Atlantic shipping lanes. Displacing over 14,000 tons she was not only larger than her
British County Class opposite numbers, she was also ten years
younger and better gunned and protected. Even the geo-
graphical positions of the opposing powers had worked to her
advantage. Forced to keep the sea for long periods so as to pro-
tect their island's supply arteries, and also maintain the
pressure of blockade, the British cruisers (built with scrupu-
lous regard to the limitations imposed by the Treaty of
Washington) had to sacrifice space that would normally have
been devoted to their protection in order to provide living-space
for their crews. But the *Hipper*, with no 'treaty' inhibitions and
possessing the attacker's choice of time and date, could house
her men ashore when not engaged in operations and thus pile
on extra armour, and engine-room power as well. Currently,
however, these advantages seemed to have little relevance.
'Offensive action' was very far from the thoughts of her commander.

When she had set out from Gotenhafen, within hours of
the *Wilhelm Gustloff*, the *Admiral Hipper* had been burdened
by over 1,700 passengers, of whom the vast majority were
soldiers, hundreds of them wounded. Outnumbering the ship's

company, their arrival had turned upside-down the *Hipper*'s
Spartan routine. Whole mess-decks had been stripped so as to
provide wards for the serious cases brought in from the front
for urgent treatment in the West, while the walking wounded
and the fit had to be content with what space they could find
in the companionways. Unemployed and hopelessly bewildered,
they seemed to be everywhere at once, and in everybody's way.
They even blocked the approaches to the guns.

It was unavoidable of course—*fortune de guerre*—and in one
sense Kapitaen Heningst was happy that his ship could be of
service to the maimed soldiers. Not only could she carry them
in quantity, she could also get them to their destination fast;
a point that, to judge by the plight of some of them, was essential. A matter of hours might stand between these men and
death. But viewed professionally the position was unpleasing
and full of complications. Just how would the *Hipper* cope in
the event of a major crisis? To what end should she give priority, should hostile forces make their appearance on the evacuation scene? The destruction of the enemy, or the security of
her passengers?

It was when the ship's officers were discussing this question,
and drawing no common conclusion on how to solve its com-
plexities, that news of the *Gustloff*'s S.O.S. was brought to the
bridge.

'*Wilhelm Gustloff* . . . torpedoed and sinking . . .'

Predictably, the first reaction was one of consternation. Why
the hell, if it *had* to happen, did it have to happen just now?
Happen when the ship was almost bursting at the seams with
her multitude of passengers! But the next reaction, equally
predictable, was to do what they could, notwithstanding.

Heningst rang immediately a change of course. The *Hipper*,
he said, would close the disaster scene at speed.

'What shall we tell our wounded?' someone queried.

'Nothing,' he answered crisply. 'There's no need for them
to know.'

As the *Hipper* changed direction, the watch was doubled and gun crews closed up—'an exercise' it was soothingly explained—while seamen off duty began once more to delve among their possessions. Already they had given much of their spare clothing to the refugees : now they began to dig out what remained for the use of the *Gustloff* survivors. Should there be any.

When Sigrid Bergfeld, still dazed by the deaths of her cabinmates and their comrades in the pool, managed to fight her way up the stairs and reach the main deck, it was to face a scene where confusion was rapidly escalating into anarchy. For some, the normal restraints on behaviour imposed by convention and courtesy had completely vanished, giving full rein to the animal impulse for self-survival. Few in number though they were as yet, these fear-driven desperadoes spared no one unfortunate enough to get in their way, and their actions were now governing the destinies of the many. A single shove would spark off a chain reaction affecting hundreds. A scrimmage at the back of the crowd would cause the centre to be transformed into a mass of dead and dying, as people tripped and fell, and were crushed by the press around them. It was a bad time for weaklings.

Meanwhile, out in the open, the task of maintaining discipline was hampered by the darkness and above all by the weather. Orders were drowned in the howl and bluster of the gale, and overall control was almost impossible to exercise. The attempt of the bridge to exert a grip on the fugitives was already breaking down, and those who tried to keep calm felt completely lost and leaderless.

The bridge personnel could get no detailed picture of the movements of the crowd or the activities of the fringe elements lurking in the shadows beyond the patchy twilight of the emergency lamps, while the ice-coated, tilting decks prevented Peter-

sen's improvised 'flying columns' from moving with the speed
that was needed to cope with local emergencies.

But if the Captain was largely ignorant of the true state of
affairs up top, the situation below decks was an almost total
mystery. Owing to the damage to the communications system it
was almost impossible to get accurate news of the exodus from
E- and F-decks, or estimate the extent of the gash the torpedoes
had scoured into the *Gustloff*'s side. Only one thing was certain :
the ship was filling fast.

Entering the cabins on F-deck through the gap opened by the
explosions, the deadweight of the water was holding shut the
inward-opening doors, trapping those who had not managed
to free themselves in the period that immediately followed the
blast. Here and there a rescue was made by seamen using axes
to smash through the door panels and extricate those inside,
but such cases were exceptional and created further hazards.
Where the doors stayed shut the occupants stayed too, until,
with the water rising, they were drowned. But where the doors
had been breached the water followed the route taken by those
who had briefly escaped it, and spilled into the interior of the
ship. Soon it was roaring along the companionways and welling
up, via the stairs, to the decks above.


It was the pressure of the numbers building up behind her,
people who in turn were under pressure from the numbers
behind *them,* the fugitives from the depths, that eventually carried Sigrid forward as on the crest of a wave, and deposited her
at a lifeboat station where some sort of order still survived under
the aegis of a group of seamen, commanded by a Leading Hand.

'Hurry along, Fraulein,' he yelled at her. 'The boat is about
to go, but there's room aboard for you.'

She listened to him, almost unbelievingly.

'Hurry up !' (a shade more impatiently). 'We're about to cast
off.'

But she didn't make it.

For suddenly she was aware of the woman who had been pushed alongside her by a further surge of the crowd. She was carrying a blanketed baby in her arms. Two small children were clinging to her skirt.

'For God's sake get a move on!' the Leading Hand implored.

Sigrid looked at him, and at the boat, and then—hardly knowing why—she stood aside.

'All right then. We'll take them,' said the Leading Hand.

When the boat began to move, the woman and her three children were aboard. It capsized the moment it touched the water. All were drowned.


'Get those bloody rafts overboard. The *Gustloff*'s not going to hang around awaiting your bloody pleasure!'

His face suffused with anger, a P.O. came up at the double, to emphasise the situation's urgency to the men at work on the floats and spur them on to maximum effort. He need not have bothered. The seamen and their soldier helpers were working as hard as any men could; it wasn't their fault that the job was taking twice as long as it would normally have done. Hacking at frozen knots with knives and axes, tearing at the ropes and wires with fingernails that snapped and bled, the squad's progress was as painful as it was frustratingly slow. The cork rafts and rubber floats and dinghies were stacked for a quick release but the weather made nonsense of the usual procedures. It was difficult even to keep a foothold on this skating rink of a deck, let alone manhandle its iced-up cargo.

Meanwhile another lifeboat had been freed: this time, the one to which Ruth Fleischer and her neighbours had been assigned. But scarcely had they begun to file aboard than a fresh crisis arose, precipitated, like its predecessor, by a batch of new arrivals crashing the queue.

'Stand back!' the seamen bawled, using their fists and boots on the rogue crowd, but even this tough reaction did little to stem the rush. Parents were parted from their children by the sheer weight of the crowd, which could hardly have halted its progress even had it tried, and panic once more claimed its quota of victims.

Three women were caught off balance as they were being helped aboard the lifeboat. They screamed all the way down, until drowned in the seething water. A seaman followed them, plummeting backwards over the side. Some later claimed that he had been hit by a crowbar, others that he had merely slipped on the ice.

In the battle for the boats a score of separate skirmishes developed, many of them bloody and none abiding by the rules. For the first time fully aware of the horror of her plight, Ruth found herself crying for help, without hope of getting it. It was then, on the verge of collapse, that she was caught in a bear-like hug, a squeeze of iron. A burly soldier had grabbed her and was forcing her forward. Momentarily she had the crazy idea that he had gone berserk—he looked so savage—but then she realised that his anger was directed at something else. The whole damn pattern of things afflicting the sinking *Gustloff*.

'You rats!' he shouted at the struggling queue-crashers. 'If I'd got my gun I'd butcher the lot of you!'

To her astonishment, the 'rats' recoiled and parted their ranks to meekly let her through.

'Hey there,' the soldier shouted, as the boat began to slide. 'Wait just a second—you've got room for one more guest!'

And next, with a splendid effort and scant care for her dignity, he had hurled her into the already crowded craft, depositing her on its occupants like a sack of coals.

'God be with you!' he said to her, and his face was lost in the crowd. Frau Fleischer was never to know the man to whom she owed her life.

## CHAPTER EIGHT

## Women and Children Last!

'WOMEN AND children to the front. The rest stay put.'

Arriving in a hurry from the bridge, the senior officer glared with incredulity and anger at the untidy scene around the boats and then, despairing of correcting it by words alone, drew his pistol as a hint that he intended to be obeyed. But the gesture was utterly wasted on the bulk of the milling crowd.

Those in the front, still trying to maintain some sort of order, were being pressed and harassed by the confused mass at their backs, a mass composed of frightened passengers blind and deaf to anything outside their immediate vicinity, and manipulated by the crush behind them.

'Stand back, or I'll shoot!' the officer threatened, but still they continued to take no notice, maintaining their massive surge towards the boat stations. As unresponsive as the tide itself to attempts at verbal persuasion, their behaviour filled him with a sense of outrage, and something approaching hate.

'I'll give you one last chance,' he said, and then, this appeal also having no effect, he fired into the air.

The immediate impact on the crowd was salutary, the whine of the bullets speaking louder, so it seemed, than exhortation. But the truce that followed was of only momentary duration, and collapsed with the arrival of yet another group of fugitives. Emerging from the entrance to the promenade deck, they re-activated the panic of their predecessors and this time the officer shot in earnest, dropping two of them. Yet even this drastic action did not stop the frantic rush; if anything, it served to make it worse.

Savage with fear after their horrific journey from the bowels of the ship, the newcomers charged head on at the boats and their guardians, and the latter were too few to hold them back. In seconds, the seamen were caught in the paralysing grasp of the mob. They had been issued with cudgels, but were so tightly enclosed that they were hardly able to move them, let alone use them. The thin line of bluejackets was broken and swept aside.

It was at this critical stage, when it looked as if the boats would be overrun, that a group of SS officers appeared on the scene. Well turned-out, and with boots and pistol belts gleaming with polish, they made no attempt to intervene but surveyed the scene detachedly, as if spectators at a zoo.

'Help us,' a P.O. cried, but they merely shrugged and turned aside, intent only on working out their own formula for escape.

'You bastards,' he yelled at them. 'You bloody bastards!' For all the good it did he might as well have saved his frozen breath.

With their heavy sea-boots slipping on the treacherous ice of the planks, and the list of the ship sending them sliding down the guard-rails, fresh reinforcements at last arrived for the hard-pressed men on the boat stations. Heads bowed against the blows of the gale, its scourge intensified by a host of bouncing hailstones, hard as pellets, they had found the going tough, exhausting not only in effort but in time.

'You've taken long enough,' grumbled the P.O. 'Why the hell weren't you here earlier?'

'You sodding well try and do the trip yourself,' came the rude reply.

Scandalised at this disrespect for rank, the P.O. wheeled angrily on the man, but then with a twinge of conscience decided to pipe down. His complaint had been unfair, and both of them knew it. Engaged on routine chores at the time the torpedoes struck, the men had been unable to start immediately for the boat-deck. They had had to go to the arms-racks for their rifles, and then fight their way back through companionways jammed by hordes of refugees before making their difficult progress along the open deck. No, they had not been laggards, nor had he thought of them as such, but when every second was vital for survival, frayed nerves triggered-off rough responses from the tongue.

'Well, now that you *are* here,' the P.O. said, 'we might inject a little sanity into this bloody mob. . . .'

It was a pious hope, but doomed to failure. It withered and died very fast—to the accompaniment of a burst from a submachine gun. But this time the shooting did not come from the sailors. Instead it was aimed at them, from figures in the shadows behind the crowd. One seaman died instantly and so did a civilian beside him. There came another spray of bullets, and these too claimed their victims.

'God Almighty!' a woman screamed. 'They'll murder the lot of us.'

There was a renewed stampede for the boats.

The identity of those responsible for this, the earliest of the shooting incidents that were to mark the passing of the *Gustloff*, is still a mystery and will probably remain so. At the time no one knew, except the guilty—and possibly only the guilty know today. The affair was localised, and occurred in semi-darkness. It was the product of a confusion in which cool heads were rare, and cool observation even rarer. Such witnesses, few in number, as survived the sinking were too shocked to obtain a truly accurate picture. Those of them, much fewer, who are still alive today look back reluctantly, and with clouded memories.

Only one thing seems clear about this astonishing fusillade, and that is the extent of its consequences. With the shots that tore into the line of bluejackets went the last attempt to control the crowd by persuasion. From then on, the sailors imposed their discipline by force.

The first sign of this changed outlook was when a large force of seamen, heavily armed, appeared on the lower promenade-deck. Neatly bisecting a fresh stream of fugitives bound like their predecessors for the boats, they pushed the rearmost ranks back into the enclosed section of the deck, and then posted themselves firmly before its plate-glass doors, forbidding exit. Almost simultaneously, another group split up into individual detachments and occupied the tops of the stairs. Petersen's plan to contain and control the crowd had at last got under way. So smartly did the men work that they had secured the routes that led to the open, and the boats, before the confused and wretched passengers had even realised what had happened. When they did, it was too late.

'We're to stop the stampede at source,' the officer in charge had told his men, and there was no doubt that they intended to follow the order through. No longer in any mood to plead with the crowd for restraint, they had taken to heart the lessons learn-ed by their comrades on the boat stations, and brandished rifles and pistols to underline their purpose. Confronted by such threatening efficiency even the worst of the tearaways came docilely to a halt.

'We'll be doomed if we stay here,' said one of them, plead-ing desperately.

'You'll be dead if you move *from* here,' a bluejacket snarled. The crowd fell back.

'Good lads,' said the leader of the team, relieved at his mis-sion's initial success. 'We've just *got* to stop any further rush for the boats and you can be as tough as you like in doing so.'

All the same, he had doubts—grave doubts—concerning the future. For the moment his men had managed to impose their grip on the crowd: for how long could they hope to maintain it? The deep interior of the ship was by now inhabited only by the waters and the dead, but there were people, hundreds of people, who, having beaten the tide, were still in transit for

the crowded deck. When they joined the thousand or more already there—the folk his cordon was currently containing—the
present atmosphere of shocked quiescence might change drama-
tically and dangerously for the worst. Each new arrival would
add to the situation's explosive content, and when flashpoint
came the consequences could be bloody.

'I'd better speak to them,' he thought, and picked up a
megaphone.

'It is essential,' he told the crowd, 'for everyone to keep calm.
There is no need for panic. Things will soon be under
control.'

From those nearest to him, and face to face with the armed
guards, there was respectful silence but scant enthusiasm. Even
as he spoke he realised that no one really believed him. However, he persevered.

'We are here,' he explained, 'on the Captain's orders, to
maintain discipline and ensure that everyone has fair play. To
rush the boats in a free-for-all means the whole rescue plan
comes unstuck, and I don't need to tell you just what *that* would
mean! If you keep your heads every one of you will be
evacuated.'

It was then, from the far fringe of the crowd, that someone
shouted, 'Bloody liar!' The officer tried hard to take no notice
and continue with his attempt at reassurance, but the voice
persisted. 'There aren't the boats available—and he knows it.
There aren't the boats to take a quarter of us . . .'

Once more the crowd began to waver ominously, and the
sailors brought their rifles to the port.

'Everyone,' insisted the officer, still disregarding the interrup-
tion, 'will obey orders and stay where they are until I give the
word to move. Any attempt to leave the deck will be met by
force. The sentries have authority to shoot to kill.'

About five minutes went by before the crowd, caught up in
one of its moods of recurrent hysteria, had occasion to experience the resolution behind his words. Two civilians, heading

a new onrush, tried to break through the cordon placed on the doors. Both of them died from the bullets of the guards.

'So let's quieten down, and be reasonable,' the officer said.

They quietened down.


Ignorant of the drama that was being played out in the enclosed section of the deck, less than two hundred feet away, Sigrid Bergfeld was an eyewitness to the consequences of panic.

Still stupefied by the tragedy that had overwhelmed the young family for whom she had sacrificed her own hope of escape, she saw to her horror yet another boat, hanging askew in the davits, suddenly race down the side of the ship and overturn as soon as it collided with the turbulent sea. And then another followed, and yet another, each of them sharing the same disastrous fate. Loosed in a hurry, and by unskilled hands, the boats hurtled into the water like falling stones, and not even the tumult of the gale could silence the screams of those aboard them.

Staring blankly at their point of impact, marked by a welter of foam, Sigrid felt very faint and terribly vulnerable. Quite suddenly it had become apparent to her that there would be no escape from the *Gustloff*—not by conventional means. There was no chance of her survival except by way of a miracle. She turned away from the guard-rail, and tried to steel herself to be brave.

Nothing, it seemed, could go right for the stricken ship. The odds were weighted against her in so many different ways that even the best efforts of those who served aboard her seemed only to aggravate the extent of the tragedy. A young officer who had maintained his section of the boat-deck as an oasis of calm and good discipline, was so conscious of his responsibility that he ordered 'Women and children *only*' when mustering the queues for the lifeboats. Only when the boat had been lowered into the water did he realise that his command had been taken far too literally. The women and children had indeed been given priority of passage, but there was no crew to row them away from the sinking ship. The sailors had all climbed out. 'Orders are orders,' the helmsman explained.

A similarly over-rigid interpretation of the 'women and children' decree nearly sealed the fate of a score or so of the wounded, evacuated from their quarters on the sun-deck. Owing to the ship's acute list it had been impossible to use stretchers to transport the men, and they had been carried to the boats in a pick-a-back style on the shoulders of fit comrades. But the P.O. in charge of the station obstinately refused to allow them to board. There was nothing in his orders, he argued, that permitted him to make special dispensation for the wounded. When a senior officer arrived to say what he thought about this blind adherence to the 'Book', the P.O. was quite offended. To have deviated from orders would have been mutinous, he said.

Following the struggle at the boat stations and the subsequent 'occupation' of the promenade deck, the passengers still at liberty in the open tended to be aimless in their direction and purpose. In small groups, they bemusedly staggered from one spot to another, each of them hopefully tagging on to the other in follow-my-leader style. Seeking salvation and not finding it, these worried folk—agitated rivulets thrown out from the mainstream of the general panic—created by their movements a state of continuous ebb and flow. For a few, however, there were more solitary beats.

Having made the open after her nightmarish escape from her wrecked cabin, Ilse Bauer had slipped on the ice and sprained her ankle. Luckily a soldier had taken compassion on her, and had helped her to a perch behind a ventilator. That, and that alone, had prevented her from being swept like many others down the steep slope of the deck and into the sea. She had taken her coat and jacket off when she had bedded down, and had arrived on deck wearing nothing more substantial than a skirt and jumper. For all the protection these gave her against

the lash of the wind and the biting hail she might just as well
have been dressed in a bathing suit.

For a few minutes the soldier stayed with her, but then said
that he must go off to get some help. He wanted to get her to a
lifeboat, he explained, but could not move her unaided : he
wouldn't be able to keep a foothold on the deck. As he pulled
off his knitted scarf and wrapped it around her neck before
lurching off to join the crowd, she was overwhelmed by the fear
that he was going to desert her. 'It's the last I'll ever see of him,'
she thought.

Numbed by the cold, and completely disregarded by the vast
concourse of people drifting around the boats and rafts, Ilse
found her new loneliness quite terrifying. At first she had been
content to remain where she was, rather than face up to the
effort required for her survival, but the mood soon changed,
and she began to cry for help. No one heard, or if they did, they
didn't care. Her voice was one of very many voices, part of the
general uproar that formed a symphonic background to the
tragedy. She was somewhat removed from the mainstream of
the fugitives, and the few who did come her way were sadly dis-
interested in her precarious plight. All of them preoccupied with
their own hopes and fears, they were disinclined to spare much
thought for others.

In the next few minutes, Ilse's panic became almost over-
powering. As the angle of the list began to steepen still further,
she wrapped her weak arms desperately around the ventilator,
convinced that otherwise she would completely slip away : go
overboard into the dreaded sea. When she suddenly discovered
that she was no longer on her own, she was so astonished that
she almost lost her grip.

'The swine !' said a female voice, with angry fervour. 'I never
thought I'd manage to get through that pack below. They've
gone mad, I tell you—completely mad. They're crazy with
fear.'

The girl was too weak, and too surprised to answer.

Elegant, and expensively dressed, the newcomer was cursing the frightened crowd with a fluency that would have done justice to a fishwife. But then her voice changed, and became compassionate. 'You're frozen, child!' she exclaimed. 'You're almost an ice-block . . .'

The teenager regarded her through frosted lashes, and then the tears came. She wanted her mother, but her mother was dead. Dead like her father, murdered at the farm. God had deserted her, and she was at a loss to know why. The woman reached over to her, seeking to console her and cuddle her back to warmth in her fur-coated arms.


Ilse was not alone in succumbing to despair. Even some of the ship's officers had become affected by it. The wild behaviour of the mob around the boats had struck severely at their morale, and the bridge was too remote to do much by way of remedy. More shocked by the lawless scenes that had followed the torpedoing than by the torpedoing itself, they felt they had lost their grip on events, and prepared for the end with a fatalism that caused them to drop out from all attempts to cope with the tragedy around them. There were, however, exceptions to the rule. . . .

One such was the gallant effort of a young lieutenant who, while the wounded were being evacuated from the sun-deck, remembered the hundreds more who were housed below, and organised a squad of volunteers to get them out. It was a brave attempt, and deserved a better fate than that which ultimately befell it. Having put their lives at hazard in their journey into the depths, the would-be rescuers found that their effort had been in vain. The companionways leading to the ward had filled with water, and the water's surface was choked with corpses. The wounded had been remembered far too late.

As the *Admiral Hipper* travelled at top speed through the dark, her passage marked only by the twin white moustaches that curved steeply upwards around the sharp nose of her bows, the scene aboard her was one of controlled efficiency and measured calm.

Extra hospital accommodation had been improvised and bedding had somehow been provided from the stores. In the galley they were preparing for a massive demand for hot coffee. Indeed, so methodical was the *Hipper*'s administration that they even diverted A.B.s to look after the children. And almost miraculously all this was being done without the bulk of the wounded even being aware of—let alone alarmed by—the ship's abrupt change of direction and objective.

The cruiser's engines were at maximum revolutions. The minesweepers that had initially accompanied her had been left behind and only the *TZ 36* was now able to keep up with her, as she travelled at twenty-eight knots through the heavy seas.

Positioned slightly ahead of the *Hipper,* the torpedo-boat destroyer had made her preparations for rescue with a thoroughness that matched the flagship's own. Scrambling nets had been rigged to help survivors climb aboard. Floats had been readied for quick release to swimmers. The crew had pooled clothes and blankets for issue to the people of the *Gustloff.* Considering the fact that *TZ 36* had been commissioned less than three months earlier, in November, and was not yet fully worked-up, her young captain, Lt-Commander Hering, had reason to be proud of his command.

Most of the ship's company were little more than boys, new recruits from the training depot, but they were all in good spirits and eager to be of service. Some had even volunteered to go overboard if need be, in order to snatch survivors from the sea. All the same, despite so much evidence of energy and effort, older hands were far from sanguine about the operation ahead. 'We're preparing to get people warmed and fed and rested,'

said one of them with characteristic cynicism, 'but most of those
we'll pick up will be fit only for burial!'

The Baltic Sea in January would have scant mercy on those
entrusted to its embrace, and the toll on the *Gustloff*'s passengers was bound to be heavy.

'You're not going to have a picnic,' said the old hands to the
young.

## CHAPTER NINE

# The Living and the Dead

IN THE steel-enclosed command bridge of the *Admiral Hipper,* heart and brain of the hurrying ship, they were reflecting not only on the problems posed by her unexpected mission but also the coincidence of its date. It was just two years short of one month since the attack on *PQ 15,* and the retreat enforced by that single British shell, but whether the omen was a gloomy one or otherwise depended on how you looked at it.

At the time of the task force's retirement, Hitler's rage had been such that he had almost contrived to scupper the cream of the surface fleet. The big ships had failed in their purpose, he'd decreed, and must be dispensed with. No longer fulfilling a useful service to the war effort, they were wasteful in manpower and material resources and should go to the scrapyard. Their armour could help relieve the steel shortage. Their guns could strengthen the coastal batteries. And their men could be dispersed into the U-boat flotillas, or else used as 'naval infantry'(!) to reinforce the army. It was a programme of almost terrifying simplicity. Had it been carried out in its entirety it would have meant, not only the end of the heavies but the finish of the Naval staff's last effort to keep 'a fleet in being'. That few of the things it threatened came to pass was due only to the diplomacy of Grand Admiral Doenitz.

Though a dedicated U-boat man, whose advocacy of the supremacy of the underwater fleet had brought him into conflict with his predecessor, the more conservative Raeder, Doenitz was too experienced a hand to believe that his cherished 'sea wolves' were sufficient in themselves to win the naval war. Should the battleships and cruisers be consigned to an early grave, then the British would no longer need to tie up vast resources to ward against surface attack on their ocean supply lines. Instead, they could concentrate their effort in one dimension alone, and turn their fleet escorts loose against the submarines.

On the other hand, the Grand Admiral—a courtier as well as a sailor—knew that to argue the point with the Fuehrer would have negative results. Even should Hitler repent his decision, he would never openly retract it. A method must be found to enable him to withdraw without appearing to : a face-saver for his infallibility.

What had finally emerged as a result of Doenitz's deliberations was a form of compromise unparalleled in previous naval history. The Battle Fleet had been 'liquidated' but the despised ships that had composed it did not end up as scrap. Instead, they were given a new lease of life, re-grouping under the euphemistic title 'Training Squadron'.

With the heavies ostensibly withdrawn from active service— although the *Tirpitz* and *Prinz Eugen* were still tacitly allowed to soldier on in Norway, the Fuehrer could be said to have had his way. But the ships themselves had survived the intended death-blow, albeit only because of the facilities they provided for training and accommodating recruits. The *Scheer, Lutzow, Hipper* and *Schleswig Holstein,* all four of them still existed, and, with them, the Battle Fleet, though under a different name.

It was just after the Russian land offensive had opened, in 1943, that the 'training ships' began to prove their worth. Containing, and rendering impotent, the bulk of the Red Fleet . . . supporting the hard-pressed soldiers in Riga, the Courland and Memel . . . the once-condemned heavies came to exert an influence that was felt throughout the length and breadth of the Baltic, and could never have been wielded by U-boats and destroyers alone. For Germany's northern garrisons, the shell that had hit the *Hipper* in that confused fight off North Cape had not been so unfortunate after all.

Now, as the raider turned shepherd sped through the night, fears and hopes were equally compounded in the minds of those aboard her.

How would their luck—the *Admiral Hipper*'s luck—work out in the test ahead?

Resignation and desperation went side by side, and expressed themselves in very eccentric ways, during what little remained of the *Wilhelm Gustloff*'s life span. At one stage, a Lutheran pastor rallied his flock around him and led them in reciting the Lord's Prayer. Then, having commended them all to the Will of God, he knelt calmly on the icy planks, his hands clasped before him; 'reconciled,' as he put it, 'for the end'. It came far sooner for him than it did for the ship. The pastor had not been on his knees for more than a few seconds before, without any warning, he pitched forward and fell. When they tried to help him up, they found that he was dead.

Another churchman was expressing *his* Christianity in a more robust style. Strongly built, he started to carry pregnant women, wounded soldiers, old folk and young children to the boats, shaming others until they followed his example, and forgot their own fright in the absorption of helping those unable to help themselves. Among them was Hilda Bendrich.

Frau Bendrich had had to climb the stairs from D-deck to C-deck in order to reach the open. Simple-sounding, the journey had brought her more harrowing experiences than the average woman would encounter in a lifetime. Carrying one daughter in her arms, she had been forced to compete for passage with men whose fear had turned them briefly into savages, without pity or chivalry as they fought their way up. The struggle had been terrifying. The worst moment of all had been

D

when she'd seen in front of her a heap of bodies, crushed beneath the weight of the panicking mob. And among them the corpses of three half-naked children. Only the need to provide for the safety of her own had enabled her to follow the tide, climbing over the dead in its *sauve qui peut* career.

But even when she reached the open deck her problems were acute. The ship's list had increased, and she was at an angle of forty degrees. For Frau Bendrich the deck took on the semblance of a glacier. Burdened as she was, she could not hope to walk up its glassy slope. The child clutched to her breasts, she could only crawl, each two yards of painful progress being followed by her slipping back one. She was on the verge of collapse when a naval officer spotted her, and detailed two soldiers to help her. It was only a matter of minutes after that before they were lifted into the waiting boat, but it seemed to Frau Bendrich that they had been wandering through an eternity.

While the pastors had been performing their acts of self-sacrifice on the sun-deck, and Frau Bendrich had been struggling towards the boat, a vastly different sort of drama had been played out in the aft end of the ship.

This began when one of the Party officials pulled a pistol from the pocket of his greatcoat, placed the muzzle at the base of his wife's head and, before anyone had a chance to stop him, shot her dead.

Aroused from frozen lethargy, a soldier rushed him, grabbed at his arm, and wrenched the pistol from him. The man offered no resistance; merely broke down in tears.

'My wife and I agreed that we would go together,' he sobbed. 'We promised we would die together. The next bullet would have been for me.'

The sailor glared at him, in a fury of rejection and disgust, then handed him back the gun. 'Here, take it, you bloody monster! Do what you want to do, and keep your side of the bargain.'

But the man's resolution wavered. He just stood there, grey-faced and trembling. 'I can't do it,' he whimpered. 'I just can't do it. Not to myself. It's quite impossible.'

'You killed *her,* the poor cow—so you'll bloody well finish the job!'

But he still couldn't, no just couldn't, steel himself sufficiently to pull the trigger.

'It's hopeless,' he pleaded. 'You don't know what it means. I just can't do it!'

They answered with jeers.

In the end, a passing officer took pity on his plight, drew his own pistol from its holster, and, shooting at short range, blasted his head off.

For Ilse Bauer, still in the warming grasp of her companion in their perch behind the ventilator, the side-effects of the chaos that had overwhelmed the ship were largely unknown. The horrors that others were forced to rub shoulders with had passed her by, and only the noise—muted by distance and seemingly having no relevance at all to her present plight—bore evidence of the disaster's mammoth scope. She was half asleep, or perhaps in a semi-coma. Nothing mattered any more, not even the cold. She just wanted to slip away, into a deep oblivion.

'Wake up! You've got to wake up!' She became aware of the voice, but tried to disregard it. Even when her shoulders were rudely shaken she was conscious of only a twinge of irritation. If she wanted to sleep, it was surely her affair. Her affair, if it came to that, if she chose to sleep forever. 'Wake up, child—you'll die if you don't,' said the voice. And this time the words were accompanied by a series of quite painful pinches and slaps.

Peevishly, her comfort shattered, the girl returned to consciousness, to see that her woman companion was now accompanied by a man. His face was oddly familiar, but she could not place why. They were staring down at her, brows furrowed with concern.

'I promised that I'd come back for you,' the soldier said.

'This gentleman is going to take you with him to the rafts,' the woman explained, then slowly, as if spelling out the words, she added 'You'll be drowned if you stay here. Drowned or frozen to death.'

'Don't know about *gentleman*,' the soldier said, with a smile of reassurance. 'But at least you'll have *some* chance if you come with us. Here you'll have none.'

'I don't want to move, I just want to be left alone . . .' But her jaws were so frozen, and her mind so confused, that they couldn't understand what she was trying to tell them.

A third party appeared, another soldier. They lifted her, disregarding her groans, and then turned to the woman. 'You're coming too?'

But she shook her head : 'I go my own way, thank you—but these may be of use to this poor child.'

She hauled off her expensive fur coat and wrapped it around the girl's shoulders. She peeled off her rings, and handed them over too. And then, before they could recover from their stupefaction let alone intervene to halt her, she had rushed down the slippery slope of the deck and hurled herself into the water.


'To all torpedo boats. Proceed to rescue survivors *Wilhelm Gustloff*. Torpedoed and sinking twelve nautical miles off Stolpemunde.'

Ever since they had received the S.O.S. the signals staff at shore HQ had been in a flurry of activity. Nor were the torpedo boats the only craft alerted by their efforts.

From Lubeck and the Hela, from Pillau and Danzig, from the haven she had so very recently left, her home port of Goten-hafen . . . it seemed that every harbour in the eastern Baltic was sending its quota of ships to the relief of the stricken liner. A cruiser, destroyers, and a shoal of smaller fry—minesweepers, patrol boats, ferries and motor launches. All were hastening, with what speed they could command, to help succour her human cargo. Even the humble dispatch-boat *VP 1703* was pressed into service. A homely, slow-moving and rather shabby little craft, she had been lying snugly alongside a Gotenhafen quayside when she had got the word to go, and though neither her skipper nor her crew could imagine that she could possibly do much good, they had slipped with alacrity, eager to have at least a try.

In spite of the overwhelming response to their urgent direc-tives and signals, there was scant complacency among the plan-ners. They were faced by a major catastrophe, and it was no use pretending that they weren't. A catastrophe that they could have prevented—if only they had believed that it could happen. When Berlin got to hear of the weakness of the *Gustloff*'s escort, heads might be expected to roll.

In the meantime, the biggest sea-disaster of all time, measured in terms of loss of life, was being staged almost beneath their noses, and all that they could do was to try and mitigate its consequences. Powerful though their efforts were, those efforts were far too late.

One of the first ships to proceed to the *Gustloff*'s aid was the Norddeutscher Lloyd liner, the *S.S. Goettingen*. But the *Goettingen*'s quick reaction had not been in response to the *Gustloff*'s signals. She had not heard the original S.O.S. and for some reason or other, had missed its retransmission as well. The first that Captain Segelken knew of there being anything untoward was when the Watch reported sighting drifting wreckage . . . planks, spars and an empty float were drifting by, and the stuff was thickening.

Strictly speaking, it was none of Segelken's business. The *Goettingen* was not a navy ship, and he most certainly was not a navy man. He had received the original U-boat Alert and, anxious to get his ship and passengers out of danger, had been travelling at speed because of it. He now sensed that the ship was nearing the area not of a small incident, but a major disaster. The time had come to throw away the rules. He slowed ship, and ordered a slight change of course, to bring the *Goettingen* even nearer to what appeared to be the centre of the trouble. Four hours of sustained effort lay ahead.

Despite the size of the operation ordered by naval HQ, and despite the extent of the area in which ships were alerted to bring aid to the stricken transport, the news of her sinking was still classified as 'Top Secret', and as such withheld from the public. But inevitably this restriction could not be maintained for long, and in general relatives and friends of the *Gustloff*'s unfortunate passengers were to hear all too soon of their loss : as loss it was to be, except for the lucky few. For some, however, there had been not even the briefest of dispensations. People in key positions had known of the tragedy almost from its onset. Among these unfortunates was Lieutenant Fleischer.

Since spelling out the Good Voyage signal to the *Gustloff* on her departure from harbour, Fleischer had been tense, and unwontedly depressed. In view of the Russians' comparative inactivity at sea he had no solid reason for his fears, and had told himself so. But all such attempts to dissipate his gloom had floundered hopelessly. Only when he heard of the ship's safe arrival in the West could he even begin to feel happy.

As communications officer of the *Lutzow* there would, of course, be ways and means of his getting this information way ahead of those obliged to rely on 'normal channels', and he planned to use his position to the full. But the hours were slow in passing, and he was in a continual fidget. When the blow fell—the blow expressed in the words on the signal pad that was handed to him from the W/T room—Fleischer felt that his world had been dissolved, and that his life was in ruins around him.

So Ruth was gone. The bride of just five days earlier had fallen victim to the merciless sea, and he, her husband, had been powerless to help her. For the first time in his experience, Fleischer plumbed the dark depths of despair. But even had he been able to get the true picture of his wife's existing plight, and had realised that not only was she still alive, but had also found a place in one of the too-scarce lifeboats, it is unlikely that he would have been very much lighter in his spirits. An open boat would be no guarantee of safety—not in this murderous weather, not in this icy sea.

## CHAPTER TEN

# The Passing of the 'Gustloff'

DULLY, only half-comprehending where she was, or how she had got there, Frau Fleischer stared at the scene around her with a sort of bewildered horror. Her reflexes were still numbed by the shock sustained from witnessing the panic on the boat-deck. She was bruised, and still part dazed, by the unceremonious way in which she had been deposited in the lifeboat, and only later did she realise the extent of the debt she owed to the anonymous soldier who had put her there. At the moment she felt too wretched to know, or even care. She considered herself to be at the whim of forces whose implacable malevolence exceeded the bounds of anything encountered in even the wildest and most frightening of nightmares. And she found herself accepting, as the obvious corollary of this, that there was nothing she could do or anyone else could do about it all, except perhaps to pray.

This mood of dumb resignation was quick to pass: giving place to alarm concerning the behaviour of the lifeboat. It was overloaded—dangerously so—yet was still continuing to linger in the shadow of the *Gustloff*'s hull. And the *Gustloff*, her decks so alive with life that she'd taken on the likeness of an ant-hill, an ant-hill savagely broken open and demolished, was tilting ever more sharply towards the sea.

'What the hell are you waiting for?' an army officer screamed at the elderly helmsman.

The man didn't answer.

'Pull away, for Christ's sake,' urged the voice of another protester. 'Pull away, you bastards, or we'll go under when she plunges.'

Though pitched on a note of hysteria, the complaint was valid enough. Even the most ignorant landlubber among the hapless survivors was aware of the danger that would confront them should the transport begin to dive. Yet the lifeboat was scarcely moving, except up and down on the swell. The *Gustloff* could well roll on top of them, or drag the boat down with her as she sank—yet here were the boat crew dallying. It didn't make sense! 'Put a jerk in it' they yelled at the helmsman.

'We've no oars!' he bawled back.

*'No oars?'*

At first, only those who were nearest the man heard his incredible statement. When, passed down the line, its meaning penetrated, their uproar gave way to an incredulous silence. The boat had no oars? They could hardly believe it.

Only later, much later, was it to become apparent that the omission was the result of an admin slip dating back to the time when the *Gustloff* had first been switched to her transport role. The boats had been requisitioned and installed in such haste that no one had noticed (or if they had, they had not broadcast it) that some of them had been supplied without their sweeps. *These,* it appears, should have been sent from another department!

'We'll just have to trust to the current,' said the helmsman.

'There's no need for panic,' added his mate. 'The current will pull us away.'

It did not require great perception on the part of their audience to realise that their confidence was forced. They were trying a brave bluff. Yet, such is the perversity of the human make up, that this latest blow served to calm rather than aggravate the mood of the survivors. Worrying, it was evident, would not serve to lessen their troubles. They could only hope for the best, and trust to luck.

A Balt launched a brave attempt to lead a small number of those around him in the Lord's Prayer, but few could hear the words through the roar of the wind and the blast of escaping steam. Nor was there any of the community hymn singing associated with the legends of other, more famous, shipwrecks. Sea-sickness, by which almost all were afflicted, acted as an effective deterrent to any attempt at song.

But whatever the wretchedness of their circumstances, and the strength of their fears, there were few of those in the boat who did not find their attention focused, almost compulsively, on the death throes of the ship. To at least one of these observers, the *Gustloff,* by then, had lost all traces of her previous identity. Indeed, she bore little resemblance to anything man-made. 'Monster of the Deep' seemed the most appropriate simile. A monster who, mortally wounded, was dying noisily and wildly; threatening, like a stricken whale, to ruin all within reach of her convulsions. She was blowing, and blowing loudly. Great jets of steam were shooting from her bowels, to dissipate in gusts in the gale-driven clouds. And she was groaning, too, her timbers crying out against the ever-increasing strain.

'She won't be long now,' the helmsman muttered. But the ship continued to delay her parting.

Less than an hour had passed since the torpedoes had struck home, but it seemed a lot longer. And still the lifeboat stayed put, as if twinned in tragedy with the tortured *Gustloff,* and destined to accompany her in her final dive to the bottom. 'We're all of us doomed,' thought Ruth Fleischer. 'It was ordained from the start.'

The first time the survivors realised that their luck might not quite have run out, was when the boat, moving in inches only from the transport's lee, was suddenly hit by a tremendous wave. It carried her, reeling, on its ice-laced crest, then hurled her violently down into the trough. The fall was so heavy that it jarred ankles and emptied stomachs. Some of the passengers were bruised, and all were shaken. Vomiting, and worse, they were thrown together in a heap—and then the boat began to climb again.

Although this served to aggravate their terror, it was followed by an awakening of hope. The progress of the boat was no longer merely vertical. Each harrowing rise and fall was followed by a horizontal drift. At last they were pulling clear of the drowning *Gustloff*'s grip.

As the minutes passed, their spirits began to revive. Sick, frozen and dazed though they were, they had managed to get the message : there was still a chance, a sporting chance, of their survival. With this feeling, however, came a belated concern for the people they had hardly dared to think of before—the people they'd left behind.

The voices of those who were still aboard the dying liner were mercifully lost in the gale, and no longer could their faces be seen, accusing and pleading. Yet somehow their presence seemed nearer than ever before. No longer rivals in the fight to escape, they could be considered by those in the boat with compassion, not unmixed with a certain sensation of guilt. Surely with hope reviving for the lifeboats, there would be hope for these, the folk left aboard the ship.

'Our people will soon be here,' the helmsman said. 'They'll get most of the crowd to safety—just you wait and see!'


Ironically, the *Gustloff*'s ending followed a brief interlude, measured only in minutes, in which a sort of calm had descended on the mass of the passengers, and optimism had begun to revive concerning their prospects.

A crop of rumours, 'inspired' or not will probably never be known, had contributed to this phenomenon. The *Gustloff*, it was whispered, had been too long a-dying to complete the job that night. By a thousand to one chance, she had wedged herself on to a sandbank—'a Ship's Officer had said so'—and would stay there, hard and fast, until the rescue was complete. Salvage

tugs were going to 'prop up' the listing ship, and passengers
would 'walk across them' to the safety of other rescue craft,
'now almost in sight'. While noticeably abstaining from posi-
tively confirming these hopeful prophecies, the officers did
nothing to contradict them, and they gained ground with incredible speed. All of them so cheerful in content and tone,
they managed to spread from mouth to mouth in seconds, and
were accepted, by some at least, as gospel fact.

But scarcely had they begun to exercise their influence on
the crowd on the promenade deck—potentially the most
troublesome of the lot—than the *Gustloff* was racked by a
sharp explosion. It arose from below, probably from the engine-
room, and was followed by a mighty groan—'a death-rattle'
as one of the survivors described it—that was heard through
the length and breadth of the ship and sent its echoes across the
sea. Spurring the swimmers to greater effort and chilling the
hearts of those in the boats, it drew from the crowd on the
Lower Promenade Deck a spontaneous yell of terror, and from
those out in the open a frantic rush for the side.

Sigrid, standing beneath the empty davits and clutching the
guard-rail, closed her eyes, let go her hold—and jumped!


'Attention, please, Attention . . .' Picking himself up from the
floor, where he had been thrown by the force of the explosion,
the officer in charge of the cordon did his best to restrain the
panic of the crowd.

'What you've just heard,' he bawled, 'was the sound of our
depth charges. We have dropped them as a precaution. . . .'

But the imaginative lie was drowned in the prevailing
clamour. 'Depth charges!' he repeated, but the words were not
even heard. And then, to finally put paid to all such attempts
at deception, another explosion followed. Nearer than the first,
it had an entirely different sound, a sound that was oddly
familiar and yet somehow out of context. Then suddenly, it was

self-evident—as the crash of breaking glass. The huge glass panels at the end of the deck had been shattered by the blow of a mighty wave, a wave that reared mountain-high above the ship, and then fell on it like a hammer. The crowd broke, and rushed for the doors. As they did so, the sailors opened fire.

It was a bloody business and as in the initial fight for the boats, the shooting was not one-sided. Once more, the sailors had their fire returned, but this time there was no budging their disciplined ranks. Neither pity nor fear could move them. They shot selectively, but shot to kill, and ceased only when the doors were blocked by the fallen.

Not everyone who fell was a victim of the bullets. The pressure of those fleeing from the onrush of the water had thrown many in the crowd off balance, and trampled them down. But the spectacle was grim indeed, sufficient to try the strongest nerve. These were their own folk. They were the very same people they normally would have been risking their lives to save. Soldiers in uniform—their comrades, had been among those who had returned their fire. Civilians, women and children among them, had been among those caught in the middle. Now, with the stampede ended and the crowd restrained, many of the bluejackets were trembling with revulsion. Despite the cold, the face of the officer was glistening with sweat.

The *Gustloff* had only minutes left, and they knew it. All of the boats, bar one, were now away. There was still a sizeable number of rafts and rubber dinghies unreleased : almost enough, though not quite enough, to have accommodated those who were still aboard the ship, but somehow this point did not matter. Had the weather been less severe, the passengers more disciplined, had the *Gustloff*'s remaining time been numbered in hours rather than minutes . . . had all these things been equal, then the fact might have been relevant, the floats put to good use and the toll reduced. As it was, however, the *Gustloff* enjoyed no such advantages. Doom was inevitable. The strained cordon . . . the cowed crowd . . . in silence they continued to face each other; uncertain, restless and sharing a mutual dread. And then, at a word, the confrontation was ended, ended on the orders of Petersen, at last admitting his ship's defeat.

With the last explosion had gone the last hope of a disciplined evacuation. No purpose could be served by further restraint. As from now, the Captain ordered, it would be each man for himself. Everything, and everyone, has a breaking point. For the ship's company, so long exposed to such desperate stress, that point was reached when they received their *sauve qui peut*. Until then, they had presented, with few exceptions, a common front, bound together by their loyalty and discipline. Individual fears had been forgotten or sublimated, in their sense of purpose. Released from their obligations, they became as vulnerable to panic as those whose panic they had fought so hard to subdue.

The last boat left in unedifying style, with stokers, deck crew and passengers fighting furiously for a place, and backing their claims with guns and bullets. It sank a minute or two later; most of its occupants were drowned.


Although initially stunned by her dive into the water, Sigrid was quick to recover her wits, and her fierce desire to live. At all costs she must somehow escape from the vicinity of the great wall that was the *Gustloff*'s tortured hull . . . the wall that, leaning towards her, threatened at any moment to overwhelm her in its fall. As the first agitated ripples of the undertow dragged at her, she struck out against the tide with a ferocity and power that, even then, she found herself marvelling at. Never before had she felt endowed with so much strength.

It was only when having swum for (what seemed to her) a considerable time, she found a drifting plank to cling on to, that she dared pause for a moment and look back. When she did so, her newfound vigour deserted her. Thrown into relief against the lights that now streamed from the *Gustloff*'s open ports and doors, people were dropping into the water in their hundreds. They could have been blobs of funnel soot, they were so numerous and so depersonalised by distance and the towering height of the ship.

As she gazed upon this panorama of disaster the girl was appalled at its nature and scope, and at her own loneliness and helplessness as well. Her nose only inches above the jagged wave crests, she hooked her arms desperately around the new-found plank, and then quite unexpectedly, she blacked out.

It may have lasted for an hour, this second period of oblivion to the horrors around her, or it may have been merely minutes; she had no means of telling. But when she came to, it was obvious that her youthful strength was failing. The cold had bitten deeply into body and brain. What drove her plight brutally home to her was when, after yet another timeless interlude she tried to move her hands, and found they would not respond. Across her torn fingernails—once so immaculately manicured, was the sheen of ice. Her hands had been frozen to the wood!

It must have been shortly after this that Sigrid first sighted the dinghy. A pale grey shade in the blackness of sea and sky, it was riding very close to her—so close that she could hardly believe the evidence of her eyes.

She tried to call out for help, but no cry came.


For Ilse Bauer the final passing of the *Gustloff* was marked by moments of unadulterated terror. Her two guardians—the soldiers who had retrieved her from her place behind the ventilator, had just turned aside to help loose one of the floats when the ship's sudden slide had sent them reeling, and cannoned her into the rail, knocking the breath from her. Momentarily she was aware of an onrush of people, running wildly towards the far side of the deck, then a wall of water rose in front of her, sweeping her off balance and, sobbing and breathless, she was engulfed by the freezing tide. It plucked her from her feet, and took her with it.

Sea water filled her mouth and overflowed into her nose and nostrils. Half out of her mind with fright she choked and retched, struggling vainly for breath and beating futilely at the white foam of the wave. A non-swimmer, she floundered helplessly, saved from drowning only by her lifejacket. Part-blinded by the water she glimpsed the scene around her only in fragmented pieces obscured by a mist of spray. There were other people in the sea besides herself, and others—hundreds of others—were jumping from the *Gustloff*'s upper deck. Instinctively she started to scream, but no help came.

Tall jets of steam were hissing upwards, framing the doomed ship like fountains before breaking and dissolving into a thin, fine rain. The rounded stern of the transport was slowly beginning to creep upward, blocking the sky. Graceless as beetles, lifeboats and rafts struggled to increase the gap between their drowning parent and themselves, traversing the wave tops in a sort of ungainly crawl.

Even Ilse, the farmer's daughter from the central plains, could see that the ship had very little time left, and divine what the *Gustloff*'s plunge would mean to those who swam around her battered hull. A deadly undertow, dragging them into the depths.

'Help me,' she pleaded. 'For God's sake help me.'

It was at that point that she realised that a sailor had overhauled her, and was swimming beside her.

'Don't give up,' he shouted. 'You'll be all right.'

But she was so cowed by the scene and so confused in her wits, that all she could do was to repeat her pleas for help, transforming them into a sort of despairing babble.

'Okay,' said the seaman. 'So *I'll* help!' But this was easier said than done.

The sea seemed determined to keep them apart. Each time he managed to get within touching distance a wave would thrust him back. Once he disappeared altogether, and her loneliness seemed more acute than ever. Yet, somehow or other, he found his way back to her, and this time closed with her, holding her tight. 'I said I'd see you all right,' he exclaimed.

Locking his arms under her armpits he towed her, struggling though she was, towards a floating plank. He eased her over it until her chest was resting on it, and abjured her harshly to hold on tight. And then, exhausted by his efforts and the cold, he slipped away, carried into the darkness in the embrace of a wave.

Breathlessly, Ilse continued to clutch on to the plank. Her prayer for help had been answered : but at the cost of a brave man's life.

Very few among the myriads who had jumped from or been swept from the *Wilhelm Gustloff* as she took her final plunge into the depths were as fortunate as Ilse Bauer in encountering would-be rescuers. Fearful of jeopardising their own chances by bringing more aboard to share their already crowded refuge, those who had managed to secure a place in the boats and floats reacted to those who cried to them for aid with hostility and even, at times, raw violence.

In one of the nastiest examples of the way in which the disaster had served to demolish even the most basic instincts of humanity and compassion, the people of an overburdened float used fists and feet to batter swimmers struggling hard to join them. For several minutes the bitter fight continued, with the besiegers increasing in numbers and desperation, and the defenders in the weight of their resistance, until finally the float itself was overturned. Dozens drowned in the ensuing panic, many of them being driven below the water by the weight of the bodies on top of them. Few rose again.

In yet another brutal conflict—this time waged around a lifeboat, seamen used sweeps and boathooks to keep survivors at bay. Terrified of the boat capsizing, they even refused to listen to the pleas of a comrade, a fellow crew member, to be allowed aboard. He called on them by their Christian names for help, but they ordered him back. When, disregarding them, he managed to get a hold of the gunwale, they smashed his hand with the back of an axe. But most of the many struggles raging in the water were between individuals, one man against another, and were fought by people who had temporarily lost their sanity.

A naval rating, swimming away from the widening vortex of the undertow, was embraced by a woman clutching hold of him in a convulsion of despair, and dragging him down with her. For a moment or two, the man tried to wriggle free and then, this and his pleadings failing, he struck at her blindly, raining blow after blow upon her until, her face a bloody mask, she loosed her grip.

Such was the sort of life and death encounter, accidental in its origins and fatal in its consequences, that made up the bulk of the struggles in the water—the reactions of people whose nerves had broken beneath the strain. In one instance, two men, colliding after their dive from the sinking ship, went completely berserk and fought each other with the ferocity of sharks. It was a fight that ended only when one of them pulled a knife from his belt and plunged it up to the hilt in his adversary's chest.

On another occasion, the occupants of a rubber dinghy, acting with rare charity, took pity on a young boy survivor and threw him a lifeline. Scarcely had he grabbed hold of it than another swimmer, a hefty soldier, pushed him violently aside, and took his place. So infuriated were the people in the dinghy at this callous behaviour that they siezed the soldier by his hair, and pushed his head under the water, holding it there until he almost died. But this rough justice didn't serve to bring back the boy. He was never seen again.

As seen from the lifeboats, the end of the *Wilhelm Gustloff* had a sort of grandeur about it—a grandeur that contrasted completely with the grisly incidents that had preceded it. To Ruth Fleischer, the way the ship made her quittance from the scene was almost Wagnerian. Momentarily, she seemed almost to right herself, exposing to their gaze the whole of her long and graceful hull and the jagged hole that marked the site of the first torpedo-hit. Obscenely disfiguring her bows it leered at them, as if mocking their efforts and their awed regard. And then, with a roar that could be heard for miles around—like a 'roll of thunder' as one survivor later described it, the ship began her death-ride.

She plunged very steeply, going down by the bows, and throwing up a debris of hatch covers, deck fittings, floats and wooden benches. She took minutes to vanish, but made her exit in style. As she slid into the water, all her lights went on again and a great scream of despair arose from those still aboard her. Horrified, the survivors watched as hundreds of figures swarmed over the light grey sides, to drop 'like so much confetti' into the seething water. The sharp stem ground itself down, disappearing from sight, and the giant propeller shafts rose in silhouette against the snow-drenched sky. Then, as this in turn vanished, a vast whirlpool spilled over the top of the ship's grave—a whirlpool that hurled its ripples so wide apart, that even the distant boats shipped water by the hundredweight and rocked and recoiled to the touch of the artificial tide. And then the sea ironed-out, and all that was left to mark the passing of the *Gustloff* was a mass of bubbles, rapidly exploded, and a litter of planks and furniture, torn from God knows where. Here and there, too, a few swimmers still survived. Not many were to last for very long.

## CHAPTER ELEVEN

# *Gesunken!*

A PITCH-BLACK sky, unrelieved by moon or star . . . a pitch-black sea that carried her down into its deepest valleys, then swept her up again on to its dizzy foam-laced crests . . . Ilse Bauer returned to consciousness to find that she was being propelled through a wild and lunatic landscape; sinister, unreal, and overwhelmingly desolate.

There was no sign of the ship, no sign of the people, and no sound at all, except for that of the sea. She was awed by the solitude that reigned around her. She might have been the only person in the universe. By now she was too tired, too numbed in mind and body, to care about what might happen to her. Even her fears had reached exhaustion-point. She was resigned to ride the journey because no alternative existed. Supported by her lifejacket and the spar, she would continue to ride the journey until she died.

Lifejacket and spar? It was only when she realised that, while the lifejacket was still keeping her head and shoulders above the waves, the spar was no longer within her grasp, that she woke to the full implications of her plight. Otherwise she might have succumbed to the fatal lethargy that had embraced her since the disappearance of the sailor. The spar that had cost a man his life to win for her, had slipped away and she had not even noticed its departure. At the thought of her loss, fresh panic sparked within her and also, perhaps perversely, the dormant will to fight.

When she saw the spar once more it was seemingly quite near. It was bobbing up and down in front of her, appearing and disappearing for long seconds at a time, but always apparently close to her. So close in fact that she thought it was well within her reach. That it was not, only became clear to her when, with a great effort, she put the matter to the test. She stretched out her hand towards the fugitive—and clutched at nothing. Slowly she began to realise that the featureless perspective, and her sad state of mind and eye, were playing tricks on her. She was seeing the spar as if in a mirage, its distance foreshortened and its outlines blurred. But still she refused to give up. Earlier, the antics of the fugitive would have left her with no sensation but that of utter helplessness, but now she found them a challenge to her cunning. At all costs, she must defeat them.

It was with a feeling of near-elation that she eventually managed to close with her quarry and grasp it to her—though 'grasp' was scarcely the word, so stiff and unfeeling were her hands. Nor did her sense of achievement survive for more than minutes. Soon she was wondering whether the struggle had been worthwhile. In one sense the spar was proving to be more of a liability than an asset. Near-drowning she had clutched at a straw, and now, subconsciously, she was placing her entire reliance on it. It was as if the fight for its possession had exhausted every remnant of her scant reserves of energy. For her 'victory' she had paid too dear a price. The coldness in her limbs was being converted into a creeping paralysis. Inch by inch, her body's life was coming to a stop. She was powerless to react to this process of deterioration. A cloud came over her brain, and she began to have little dreams. In a brief moment of lucidity, she managed to think : 'I will die if I stay like this. I must start moving off on my own.' But when she tried to let go of the spar, she found that she could not. It was her only link with things man-made, things of the land, and her only companion in these untenanted wastes. She could not lose it.

A long interval passed in which she felt precisely nothing; not even cold or pain. But the little dreams expanded into big dreams, and these in turn became hallucinations. The struggle aboard the ship, the harsh embrace of the sea had had an effect upon her that was truly traumatic. The suicide of the woman who had given her the coat, the disappearance of the soldiers who had tried to help her to the rafts, the drowning of the swimmer who had secured the spar . . . all who had given her aid had met with a tragic ending. Her cat-naps became things of terror. . . .

When the girl first saw the float she was content to just look at it, but she didn't believe it. It wasn't real, *could* not be real— just another product of the disorder in her brain. Even when she saw the faces peering down at her, and watched their lips form words, she refused to believe that she was once more in the company of her kind. She was not to be fooled, not this time, into turning for help to phantoms.


The two seamen in charge of the float had great difficulty in hauling the girl inboard. She seemed incapable of making any effort to assist them and her body was so much deadweight. What further hampered them was the texture of the coat that she was wearing. Its expensive fur had probably served excellently in keeping out the very worst of the cold, but it was hard to handle after its long immersion in the freezing water. The once soft and flexible surface of the garment was now hard and slippery as the ice that covered like a sheet its separate hairs. At one time the girl escaped their grasp altogether, and fell back into the sea. When they eventually retrieved her from the water, and hauled her inboard to join the rest of their flock, the seamen were acutely aware that their job was only half done. Restoring the girl's circulation and rousing her from her semi-coma proved difficult enough, but it looked like being simplicity itself when contrasted with the need to soothe her fears and heal her shock. For this, they were ill-cast, and ill-equipped as well. Sick with their own apprehension and the cold, they were in no great shape to improve the morale of others. But, however inadequately, they attempted to do their best. Most of those around them had experienced for themselves, though to a lesser degree, the sort of ordeal that Ilse had endured. Even the few who had been aboard the float since the time of its launching were in scarcely less discomfort and hazard than those who had managed to reach it only after a swim. Repeatedly the sea swept over them. Their clothes were sodden, and their limbs were frozen.

'You're in luck, Fraulein,' said one of the seamen in an attempt to reassure their latest 'catch', returning slowly to life. 'While other poor devils struggle in the drink, all we've got to do is wait. The Navy will get us off in next to no time.'

Yet behind the brave words, the thought must have been lurking: 'Yes, if they find us soon. For if they don't, then you, and us, will have had it.' Not many would be able to hold out until dawn.


Sigrid's tongue, swollen and immovable, was filling her frozen mouth and throat: she could not even raise a croak. She was terrified lest the people in the dinghy would not see her, or that, if they did, they wouldn't pick her up but, preoccupied solely with their own survival prospects, would ignore her and let her drift by in the dark.

A few hours earlier, this latter fear would have been unthinkable to the idealistic young helf, reared and educated in the traditions of German chivalry and self-sacrifice; the 'gentlemen folk' would surely not desert her! But the scenes of frenzy aboard the *Gustloff* had administered a monumental shock to all that, until then, she had accepted and believed in. Say the people in the dinghy were cramped for space, and decided that one more survivor would worsen their own doubtful chance of rescue? Say they refused to take her? At thought of losing contact with her own, and being left to drift to her separate destiny, her fears became unbearable and ungovernable. Again she tried vainly to scream.

It was then that she discovered that an arm was locked round her own and that slowly, ever so slowly, she was being lifted from the water. Then she became aware that something solid was beneath her feet, and that a ring of faces surrounded her. Mere shadowy blurs in the darkness, but the faces of her kind.

'She's still alive,' said someone. It was a gruff voice, uncultivated, but oh, so lovely!

It was some time later, when she had returned to full consciousness, that the girl began to realise that the security afforded by the dinghy was largely illusory. Her refuge provided a perch as comfortless and almost as bleak as the cold sea itself. Her companions were six in number, two women and four soldiers. They seemed glad to have her with them, but made little demonstration. Except for the man who had helped her aboard, they hardly spoke : not surprising, since in the circumstances in which they found themselves, speaking would have been an expensive process, exhausting in its demands upon their energy, of which there was little left. With shoulders slumped and eyelids closed, they were bunched together, seeking warmth but not finding it, and oppressed by their thoughts.

The wind was as bitter as ever, although the hail had stopped. The water the dinghy had shipped had turned into a lining of ice. As the minutes passed, Sigrid began to feel even colder than she had been in the sea. Her uniform skirt and blouse—they had once been described as 'saucy'—were frozen solid and enclosed her limbs above the knees in glittering armour. Her legs had no feeling at all and were incapable of movement. Once more her brain began to play her tricks.

The lifeboat that had Ruth Fleischer among its passengers was so hopelessly overloaded that it seemed doubtful if it could survive for very long. Even at the best of times the restless water was within inches of the gunwales. At the worst, the boat was shipping the stuff by the tubful. Its occupants, sixty or more of them, had long since been drenched to the skin. Now, to add to their accumulated misery, the icy spray, whipped inboard by the wind, burst on them like miniature shrapnel, blinding them.

Following the disappearance of the *Gustloff*, their spirits had sunk to zero. Few of them tried any longer to strike even a pretence of hope. Although Ruth, for one, was almost unable to move—so tightly was she confined by the bodies of those around her, she was vaguely grateful for the way in which they served to blunt by a fraction the sharp edge of the wind, though even this could not prevent her from shaking. At first, copying the example of her near-neighbours, she had stamped her feet up and down on the duckboards, and had clenched and unclenched her fists to keep the circulation going. But her limbs, despite this 'exercise', had now ceased to have any feeling, and she could no longer control them. Her brain seemed frozen, too.

Soldiers, VIPs, peasants . . . men, women and children . . . the protests, chit-chat and groans of her fellow passengers had been silenced. Huddled together, they had little in common except the bond of their collective suffering—that, and their jealous resolve to keep their wretched refuge for themselves. Had they not had to fight for their places in the lifeboat it is possible that their immediate reaction to the fate of those who the *Gustloff*'s passing had left struggling in the water would have been less negative than it was. Had not the oars been missing it is possible that they might even have attempted to do something by way of rescue. As things were, however, they thought it just as well that the boat should be so reliant on the vagaries of the tide. Once among the drowning, they might have shared the drowning's fate.

Yet here and there were odd exceptions to the mood—the

mood that held the majority preoccupied only in ensuring their own survival. One such was the exemplary behaviour of the naval helmsman, still trying, though noticeably less energetically than before, to inject a note of cheer into his charges. Another, was the general solicitude shown for three small children who had lost their parents in the sinking. If ever anyone was in need of comfort those kids were, and even the comfortless turned their attention to them, though small good did it appear to do in alleviating their shocked misery.

Among the orphans was an eleven-year-old boy whose mother had overbalanced when she had tried to follow him into the boat. Falling into the water, she had been swept away and drowned. At the time, the boy's grief for his mother had been such that he had had to be physically restrained from throwing himself in after her. Now he was sobbing bitterly into the coat of the man who had held him back, the man from whom he had recently been fighting to free himself. Ruth Fleischer was by no means the only person in the boat to feel guiltily glad that the sound of the wind and the sea served to deaden his pathetic and harrowing cries.

Apart from this sad little drama, and the need to divert the two younger children, rescued by a sailor when their parents had been trampled down in the rush for the promenade deck, there was little to catch the attention of the people in the boat or distract them from their morbid lethargy. At odd intervals only would they show a brief sign of interest, notably on those occasions when one of the crew members fired a flare. As it soared upwards, hissing and crackling, to spread its scarlet blossoms across the sky they would rouse themselves from their trance and anxiously scan the horizon, searching for a sign that rescue was on its way. But each time their curiosity was unrewarded by results, and died as quickly as the flare itself, fading, falling and extinguished in the sea.

It was after one of those frustrating episodes of half-hope followed by bitter anti-climax, that Ruth, roused from a brief sleep shot with delirium, first heard the voice. It came from the darkness—more total than ever following the flare's demise—and seemed to be fairly close.

'Boat ahoy! We need help . . .'

But no one answered.

'Help,' the voice repeated. 'For God's sake help us!'

This time it was answered by a gruff warning to keep away.

Uncomprehendingly, Ruth peered outboard, to see what at first appeared to be a mound of debris floating on the water. On a second look, however, this resolved itself into an upturned dinghy. A man was clinging to it and, as she watched there came from him yet another desperate plea for aid. Like its predecessors, it met with scant sympathy.

'We've no room for you,' one of the seamen yelled back. 'The boat's overloaded already. She's topheavy with people and ice.'

Shocked, Ruth suddenly felt obliged to speak. 'We can't refuse him,' she protested to those around her. 'We surely can't leave him to drown!' But it was evident that her audience did not share her qualms.

'Fraulein, you don't understand,' her neighbour retorted indignantly. 'It's a question of them or us.' And then he added, in a slightly gentler tone: 'This old tub is hopelessly overcrowded. If we try to take any more aboard, she'll turn over and go upside down!'

Intimidated into silence, though ashamed of being so, the girl cast another worried glance towards the capsized float. The man had detached himself from it, and was beginning to swim towards the boat. He was swimming very oddly, as though towing something behind him.

'I said, keep your distance!' warned the seaman, but the swimmer, taking no notice, continued to come on until at last he managed to get alongside and clutch with his left hand one of the empty rowlocks.

'I've got my wife here,' he pleaded. 'You surely can't let her drown.'

'Your wife!'

Suddenly they were aware that the shapeless object he was towing was a woman—a woman in the last stages of collapse. He was holding her with his right arm thrust through the strings of her lifejacket. As the swell bounced her against the side of the boat, she raised her face and groaned.

'For God's sake take her aboard,' the man begged. 'She'll bloody well drown if you don't.'

But they still did not budge . . .

It was a young soldier who broke through the hard crust of their unnatural indifference, and reminded them, as he did so, of their temporarily lost humanity. Unexpectedly rising from his seat, he faced the crowd belligerently, as if challenging them to fight, and then, turning from them with an expression of disgust, he yelled to the swimmers: 'We'll have you.'

In grave danger of overbalancing, he threw his body over the thwarts, reached out his hands for the woman, and with a mighty heave pulled her aboard like a landed fish, depositing her almost in Ruth Fleischer's lap.

'That's *that*!' he said roughly, and then grabbed hold of the man. Seconds later he, too, was safely aboard.

The crowd looked at the rescued couple, then at the soldier —and then they glanced at each other, and fell silent, as if ashamed.

## CHAPTER TWELVE

## The Frozen Sea

IT WAS full house on the command bridge of the *Admiral Hipper* as she neared the disaster area. The *Gustloff* had vanished, and so had the moon, but Heningst didn't need the calculations of his chartroom to establish that the cruiser was dead on course for the scene of the sinking.

A good twenty minutes had passed since 'distress signals ahead to starboard' had been reported from the masthead, and the officers had sighted through their night-glasses the flares sent up by the victim's lifeboats rising high above the sealine—red embers in the blackness. Now the first fragments of the wrack that the tragedy had left behind were rolling by, glimpsed dimly against the white of the *Hipper*'s bubbling wake. To many of the ship's company this was the near-culmination of the cruiser's dash to the rescue, and morale soared high. But Heningst knew that it was, in fact, only the beginning. Never before in the history of the sea had there been a disaster of such magnitude in terms of human life. And seldom before had would-be rescuers been faced with such a variety of problems: problems of navigation, tests of decision and will. He, for one, had no illusions about their intricacy and extent.

First there was the danger that the *Hipper*'s arrival might prove more of a curse than a blessing to those she had come to save. Without the nicest seamanship in her timing and handling, the cruiser could blunder like a rogue elephant into the mass of the survivors, her armoured bows carving into lifeboats and rafts, and her spinning screws slicing the swimmers into shreds.

And then there was the menace of submarine attack, with the possibility that the ship might herself end up as victim. To stop the *Hipper,* or even to slow her, in these circumstances would offend even the most basic principles governing the handling of a major warship. And yet, if the *Hipper* was not to stop, or slow, there could be no rescue; no hope for the *Gustloff*'s survivors.

Outwardly almost impassive, but inwardly acutely aware of the grave risks he was taking, Heningst announced to the bridge his big decision. The *Gustloff*'s boats would not fall victim to the cruiser's wake, and neither would the swimmers be left to drift away in the dark. He would light up the scene, and risk the enemy's attention. The ship would switch on her searchlights, and slow speed as well.

'Because of the submarine danger, *Hipper* was not in a position to take part in the rescue of the swimmers from the *Gustloff*, and left the area with her 1,500 wounded, heading west.'

This laconic statement is the only reference made in the German official history of the war at sea to *Hipper*'s behaviour during the aftermath of the *Gustloff*'s sinking. It is a reference that—say those who served on the cruiser at the time—does her far less than justice, and Heningst no justice at all. It fails completely to mention the strenuous efforts he had ordered, efforts in which every member of the ship's company had enthusiastically joined, to prepare his command for a massive intake of survivors. Nor is there any hint of the way in which the *Hipper* changed course to reach the scene, and the considerable risks she ran in doing so. But the greatest cause of offence is the book's omission of the practical difficulties that stood in the way of lifting the survivors—difficulties that were to prove insurmountable.

'For all that history has to say about our ship's response to
the *Gustloff*'s call for help, you'd think she behaved as casual-
ly as the priest and the levite,' an ex-*Hipper* Leading Seaman
has since put it. 'But of course, she did nothing of the sort.
You've no idea of the problems involved in trying to use a ship
of such size and weight as a rescue craft, able to nip in and out
of the hordes of people and rafts in the water. For all the service
she was able to afford, and for all the credit she got, the *Hipper*
might as well have never tried at all. . . .'

From the very beginning, the cruiser's attempted intervention was dogged by misunderstanding. The dazzling glare of
her searchlights brought not hope, but terror, to the swimmers.
Instead of a cheer, a cry of fear went up : 'The Russians!' someone yelled, and the word spread like an infection.

The ship's outline was distinctive enough; so distinctive as
to be almost unmistakable. The trouble was, no one could see
her : she was, of course, invisible behind the blinding light.

'It's the Russians!' In fear of massacre, people began to slip
from the boats and rafts—conspicuous targets, surely, for the
bolshevik gunners!—and scattered willy-nilly across the sea.
Useless for the helmsmen to holler, as did the helmsman of the
boat that carried Ruth Fleischer, that they were merely hastening the end they feared—death in the embrace of the freezing
water. To many the word 'Russian' had been a bogey for so
long that the very sound of it sparked off a mindless hysteria,
an impulse for self-destruction as old as that of the Gadarene
swine. It was only when, instead of shells and bullets, a voice
came echoing across the noise of the gale, a voice amplified a
hundredfold by the *Hipper*'s tannoy, that the mood of the multitude returned to sanity, and panic changed to exaggerated hope.

'Help has arrived,' proclaimed the voice. 'So hang on all of
you. Help has arrived. This is the *Admiral Hipper*!'

The *Admiral Hipper*. 'The Lucky Ship'. The very name
reassured them.

'Help has arrived,' the voice repeated, and this time they *did* raise a cheer, even though it was one that was faint, a reflection of their exhaustion. They had no idea that the cruiser's efforts were to prove completely futile. Nor that she was not with them to stay.

The 'difficulties' that beset the rescue-bid were greater than even Heningst had anticipated. In the end, they were to defeat him.

The ship's high freeboard was a major obstacle to lifting the survivors, as it ruled out direct physical contact between them and the deck parties. The swimmers were too exhausted to make use of the lines that were thrown to them, and there was no hope of hand grasping hand across the gulf between the waves and the cruiser's main-deck. The vast steel protuberances from the *Hipper*'s side that represented the turrets housing her secondary armament of 5.9s and flak guns, gave rise to further snags. Preventing the deployment of scrambling nets, the turrets canalised the rescue effort into narrow channels and the survivors were so frozen that they could not grasp, let alone climb, the rope-ladders that had been dropped from less cluttered areas of the deck.

Again, the *Hipper* was far too large to manoeuvre herself alongside the packed lifeboats, and the boats were too small or, rather, too thin-skinned, to risk coming too close to their 'rescuer'. Even had their crews the energy—and this they had not—to tackle the tricky job of bringing them in, such a move would have served no purpose. At a single touch, the heavy swell could have dashed them and cracked them against the armour of the hull.

As the minutes passed without any tangible result, and frustration steadily mounted, Heningst reluctantly came to the conclusion that the weakness of the survivors was so acute as to rule out all hope of success for the original rescue routine. The only way of getting the swimmers inboard was to go out and fetch them. Although there was no shortage of volunteers it was obvious that even this last desperate resort could save only a minute fraction of those struggling in the water.

'We'll do what we can,' said Heningst, 'but the chances are very slim.'

As picked seamen climbed down the ice-crusted ladders to position themselves for their task—a back-breaking and time-consuming process in which each individual swimmer would have to be lifted from the water and passed up to the deck by a human chain, Heningst turned once more to his individual battle. On the one side was his instinct, as a sailor, urging him to perservere, even against all hope, in this effort to save those menaced by the common enemy, the sea. On the other was his responsibility as a naval officer for his ship : a ship, moreover, that was one of the largest major units in his country's depleted fleet. The *Hipper* could not stay on the scene forever.

'U-boat contact !'

'You're certain of that?' queried Hering.

But the asdic operator was adamant. 'Positive contact, sir. One hundred percent.'

'The Devil !'

Hering, on the cramped bridge of the destroyer, involuntarily cast a glance to port, and the source of the searching pencils of light that swept the *Gustloff*'s survivors. Did *Hipper* know? It was essential that she did. 'Send a signal,' he began, but the order was superfluous. The heavy cruiser, too, had registered 'positive' and was reacting at speed. The searchlights went out, and, her movements unseen but guessed at by her consort, the *Admiral Hipper* began to turn. Not just one submarine, but submarines. Submarines in vast numbers !

Heningst had winced as he'd received the U-boat warning. The moment he had so much anticipated and dreaded was now upon him. The moment of choice.

Outside the ship, the hundreds in the water unaware of this

E

shift of chance, were still looking to the *Hipper* for safe refuge. But inside were the fifteen hundred wounded, plus the members of the ship's company, almost as many more again. Torn by his loyalties, as he saw it his duty was plain. Slowed as she was, the *Admiral Hipper* would be a sitting duck for the enemy's torpedoes. Even at speed she had no hope of hitting back. Nor could her escort do much that was effective : commissioned only three months earlier, she was scarcely worked up as yet, and the bulk of her crew was composed of young recruits gaining seafaring experience. Even had she been twice her size and weight, and a battle-hardened veteran as well, the *TZ 36* would have presented little menace to the Russians in the current circumstances. To use her few depth charges when the water was crowded with survivors would massacre the very people she was endeavouring to save. And the limitations imposed by this daunting fact applied, needless to say, to the *Hipper* herself. Even evasive action on her part would create havoc among the *Gustloff's* drifting multitude. No, Heningst decided, there really was no help for it. He would leave the escort behind, to do whatever she could, but the cruiser must break off the rescue and resume her original mission. She had risked too much, for too long, and had achieved almost nothing by doing so.

'Full ahead both !'

As he gave the terse command that was to mean retreat for the *Admiral Hipper,* and send her racing to the safety of the west, her captain's face was expressionless and his voice was calm. But he kept his head high, and his eyes to his front, staring into the blackness as if at some invisible horizon. Maybe, they surmised on the command bridge, he just hated to look down. Maybe, he dreaded seeing the crowd the ship had left behind her.


The bright searchlights of the *Hipper* had reached far into the night, but they never touched the float that carried Ilse Bauer.

It had been swept by the tide a long way from the grave of the *Gustloff*. Beyond the outer fringe of the swimmers and the wreckage it rose and fell on the swell; a little world of its own, a frozen world. Although so divorced by distance from those who had struck out towards the cruiser expecting to be taken aboard, the people on the float had shared their hope.

'Must be a *big* ship,' one of them had croaked. 'She *must* be big. You can tell by the size of her lights.'

But would she see them?

'Where there's one, there'll be many more,' said the optimist, ignoring the question. 'When the daylight comes, the sea will be alive with ships.'

When daylight comes! Day seemed a long way off—could literally be an eternity away. At thought of it, their spirits slumped again.

Burrowing deeper into her 'legacy', the fur coat, Ilse briefly wondered how others on the float, less well-endowed, could possibly survive the freezing night. Even with the coat's protection, she could not stop her limbs from shaking, and when she moved her cheek muscles it was with pain and effort. The taut skin over her cheekbones felt as if it would crack. In sudden panic, she found herself praying. Dear God, the ship *must* see them. Must somehow pick them up. They could not wait until daylight. They couldn't *live* that long!

'Why doesn't she launch her lifeboats? Why doesn't she search for us?' It was an effort even to frame the petulant question. Her frozen lips turned it into near-gibberish. And then, as she waited for an answer, the friendly searchlight beams vanished.

'It's only temporary. A security precaution. They'll switch them on again in a minute. . . .' But even the optimist spoke without conviction. The blackness now seemed more intense than ever. Even the distant flares seemed to lose themselves in the vast maw of the night. On the float, the sense of loneliness was total.

Huddling together, in desperate search for comfort, they stared with aching eyes towards the spot where the lights had been as if mute supplication could bring them back again. But nothing happened.

'The bastard! Oh, the bastard! She's run away and left us. . . .'

It was the former optimist speaking. Ilse burst into tears.


When the *Hipper* had turned away, the people in the lifeboat had felt that their blood was ebbing in her wake. They were sure that her escort would go with her, and that they would be left to their fate. But even should the destroyer stay behind, their chances, they knew, would be slim. The *TZ 36* could not be everywhere at once, and she would be giving first priority to the swimmers. Daylight would bring search aircraft and more ships. But daylight was still several hours away. By daylight they would be dead.

They had shared to the full the apprehension of the other survivors at first sight of the *Hipper*'s searchlight and had experienced also the joyous intoxication that had followed the announcement of her identity. Now the stark contrast between that moment of grateful optimism and its cruel, contradictory climax was too much to bear. Not everyone in the boat was so uninformed about the principles governing the conduct of naval ships at war as not to realise that there was good reason for the cruiser's hurry, but that reason was not one to freely broadcast, or from which to derive much comfort. Who wanted to be told that the U-boat that had struck the death-blow to the *Gustloff* was still in the area, and looking for fresh victims? Worse, that she probably had fellow hunters with her?

Thus, while the ignorant might curse the *Hipper*, as cowardly abandoning them to their fate, those in the know found in their knowledge only an additional cause for fear. Friendless, they were at the mercy of their enemies.

The three orphans were still whimpering, but efforts to comfort them had fizzled out. Even the man at the helm had abandoned his forced attempt at optimism. Glumly, heads bowed against the gale, he and his mate no longer abjured their charges not to worry. Their confidence had vanished with the cruiser.

On the *TZ 36* they felt rather lonely too. The departure of the *Hipper* had come as quite a shock, even though they guessed the reason for it. Starkly emphasising their own vulnerability, the move was one they didn't much care to think about, but think about it they did, nowithstanding. For Hering the rescue battle must now be fought on two fronts: against a human enemy as well as against the sea. For the latter, he had already made his preparations, confident that the highly manoeuverable and low-lying destroyer was likely to succeed where her massive consort had failed. For the former, the fight against the U-boat, it would be a question of skill; the skill of a handful of trained technicians, in the asdic and radar teams, and his own capacity to think just slightly ahead of the enemy commander.

To assist him to defend the ship in her mission of mercy he detailed just over a quarter of her crew to act as lookouts, messengers, engine-room staff and gun-crews. The rest, he assigned to the rescue proper. Even then, he reasoned, they would have their work cut out. Already some of the survivors had been grabbed and lifted inboard by members of the ship's company. Now began the second, and most daunting phase of the operation—a descent into the sea to reach the swimmers.

Burdened as they were by their heavy seaboots and oilskins, the young sailors could scarcely be described as agile, but they reacted smartly to their orders, and showed no signs of holding back. Sliding over the side, to cling like clumsy spiders in the web of the scrambling-nets, they had a task that no veteran would have envied, and quite a few would have baulked at, and that they did it at all, let alone did it well, was to surprise them, but only when it was over.

'At the time it was happening,' one of them was to recall,

'we worked as if anaesthetised, or under the influence of drugs. After the first few minutes, even the bite of the cold had ceased to matter. You no longer cared. There was never a moment to spare, no pause for thinking. You lost all sensation, except the need to keep going.'

There was little that was haphazard about the rescue plan, and no half-measures in the way it was carried out. A detachment of sailors balanced themselves on the lower rung of the nets, and with their legs awash in the icy water, hauled in the survivors one by one, lashing them to the nets to prevent them falling back into the sea. Then, while they fished around for other swimmers, another detachment of rescuers hoisted the survivors a stage higher, until the deck crew 'landed' them, escorting them into the warm interior of the ship.

It was a well thought-out procedure, and it worked. Even though there were plenty of snags to slow it down. Not the least of these was the dead weight of some of the rescued. Semi-conscious, they were difficult to lift, and difficult to hold on the ascent. Again, there were bottlenecks in the procedure as the deck became more cluttered with those who, once inboard, simply collapsed, and had to be carried below.

Time after time, the weakened survivors dragged from the sea by the men at the foot of the scrambling-net literally slipped through the hands of the rescuers, falling back into the water before they could be lashed to the rungs. Time and time again, the young sailors had to dive in after them to retrieve them, only to emerge as frozen and exhausted as those they had saved. People who, in a revival of panic, tried to 'rush the queue' also created hindrance to the plan, but the biggest problem of all was posed by the ship's shortage of living space.

With this factor in mind, Hering had ordered that priority in rescue should be given to the people in the water. Those in the boats would have to wait for another ship. But when it was discovered that two of the boats (incidentally, the best-disciplined) were filled with women and wounded an exception had to be made, and this one 'exception' created several more. Soon every foot of the *TZ 36*'s interior was occupied. There were survivors in the companionways, the messes, even in the engine-room. Among them was Ruth Fleischer, more dead than alive, and the people from the lifeboat, almost incoherent in their gratitude. The ship was stretched wide, and could not be stretched much more. Yet still Hering refused to leave the scene. Hundreds were now aboard the small destroyer, but hundreds more were still in the water, crying for aid. *TZ 36* must soldier on.

Since the very start of the operation he had stayed on the bridge, leaving others to fight the battle against the sea and concentrating instead on thwarting the other enemy; the enemy who was lurking on the fringe of the rescue area, and biding his time. So far the *TZ 36* had lifted nearly four hundred people, but how many more could she afford to house? How many more would she be allowed to take aboard before the submarine, no longer content with watching, would feel that the moment was ripe for her to attack?

'The U-boat is beginning to move, sir.' The asdic operator's warning cut sharply into Hering's reverie, confirming his fears. But he answered merely: 'Very good.'

'She has started her engines, sir—and is beginning to turn, bows-on.'

So this was it! The Russian was manoeuvring to aim his torpedoes, and catch the ship broadside on.

Hering said: 'Very good. When she turns, we'll turn with her. . . .'

## CHAPTER THIRTEEN

## *When Death Passed By*

'U-BOAT making a 35 degree turn, sir!'

'Turn 35 degrees,' said Hering through the speaking-tube. The *TZ 36* began to swing round, to present her stern to the enemy.

'Well, at least he'll know we've rumbled him,' said Hering.

At all costs the ship must not be caught broadside on. Every degree turn of the submarine must be countered by a corresponding turn, a follow-my-leader exercise in which the 'leader's' moves could be traced only by the pattern of the 'pings' in the asdic operator's earphones.

'U-boat turning again, sir.'

Once more the destroyer swung to the enemy's course, and the incredible rescue continued. But how long could her luck last? Certainly not for ever. Idly Hering wondered what they were thinking about it below, and came to the wry conclusion that they must be feeling pretty good. Encumbered as she was, and semi-blind, the *TZ 36* was at a considerable disadvantage. And the Russian commander must know it, be confident of a breaking point.

On the bridge they were gripped by a tension that dulled them to all but the work in hand. Oblivious to the shouts of the rescued and the swimmers, and the clatter along the deck as a new batch of shocked and frozen survivors was brought aboard, they had ears only for the sing-song phrases from the chart-room, giving the enemy's position and depth and estimating the extent of every turn. It was an eerie duel, this battle of wits between ship and submarine, and a complete reversal of their normal tactical roles. With a clear sea, and a trained crew, it would be the *TZ 36* that played the part of the hunter. As it was, she had been transformed into the hunted. But for how long could the guessing game be confined to just two players? In his mind's eye, Hering could see a very disturbing picture—of other 'Ivans' homing-in on the scene. But he'd stay for as long as he could. . . .

'A second U-boat! Port ninety degrees.'

The warning that put an end to the destroyer's effort was inspired not by the asdic but by radar.

A submarine, only partly submerged, was jostling for position on the ship's port quarter. The *TZ 36* was being sandwiched between two enemies. A minute's delay could be fatal.

'Full ahead both,' Hering ordered.

At the jangle of the telegraph the little ship bounded forward, throwing the crowded decks into momentary chaos, and sweeping the swimmers aside with the violence of her wake. As she did so, two pencils of white foam shot through the troubled water, overhauling her. One torpedo passed her to port, and one to starboard. And, hardly believing her own good fortune, *TZ 36* ran at maximum revs for home.


Kept unaware of the drama that was being enacted on the bridge, and oblivious to the meaning of the frothing bubbles that marked the torpedoes' passage, the refugees from the *Gustloff* were grateful for small mercies, which were all that the destroyer could provide. Hot coffee by the gallon, scores of gallons—in the galley the cooks, reinforced by volunteers, were working themselves silly in their efforts to meet the demand. Anything, but *anything,* was good for the shocked survivors, provided it could bring to them some degree of warmth. To stretch the ration, the coffee had to be liberally watered-down,

E*

but however ersatz the 'ersatz', it did not prevent it from being welcome.

In the small sick-bay too, and its extension in the wardroom, there was work in plenty to be done as the ship raced for base; although some of the cases that they had to cope with would have been rare, to say the least, in a peacetime navy.

When Ruth Fleischer had been brought aboard her case was considered simple—but 'simple' only in the sense that there were so many far worse-off than she. The condition that had entailed her having to be carried from the boat—frostbite in both legs—was one that they were trained and equipped to remedy. Even the wounded soldiers presented few complications, except for those arising from their numbers when contrasted with the little ship's scant medical resources.

It was when confronted by a vastly different sort of patient that the sick-bay's confidence began to falter. In lifting the *Gustloff* passengers, a top-priority had been given to pregnant women, 'for self-inflicted wounds' it was wryly explained at the time. Now one of them, to the horror of the SBA and his over-taxed comrades, showed every sign of giving immediate birth.

'Can't she wait until we get to base?' protested the First Lieutenant, scandalised.

But she couldn't, and meanwhile the news spread like wildfire through the ship. Was a new life to emerge, in the wake of the *Gustloff*'s wreck? Or was this to be yet another hope destroyed? Would the mother, having lived through the ordeal of the sinking and its aftermath, contrive to survive this further hazard? Or was this to be, with wicked irony, the mortal blow? The health of the mother and the child-to-be rapidly became a major talking-point on the *TZ 36*. To the team in the sick-bay, however, it was rather more than that.

A major challenge on unfamiliar ground, they accepted it with embarrassment, and reluctance. They were abashed by the responsibility it imposed on them; they who knew so well the extent of their limitations. In the end, however, they rose nobly to the occasion, and more than justified the reputation enjoyed by sailors the world over for adaptability and resource. Assisted by a nurse who had survived the *Gustloff's* sinking, they produced the child, saved the mother, and united their role as midwives with that of godparents too.

'That won't shake a sailor,' the old ballad goes; that they *had* been a trifle shaken, the sick-bay sailors never showed. When they made their triumphant announcement, everyone brightened up. Even Hering, still on the bridge, briefly broke his vigil against the foe to express his pleasure at this small glimpse of sunshine in the gloom and send his felicitations to the mother. They'd wet the baby's head when the ship entered harbour. . . .

For the *TZ 36* the voyage was nearly over; for the survivors aboard her a night of terror was drawing to its close. Not so blessed was the lot of those she had been forced to leave behind : those of them who were still alive.


Ilse Bauer, mercifully ignorant of the arrival of the Russian reinforcements and the reason why the destroyer's rescue bid had ended, found it impossible to sleep, or even to doze. In this, she was an exception. Everyone else on the float had succumbed to the bludgeon of the cold. So many blurred outlines only a shade lighter than the sea, they were either asleep or unconscious : she didn't know which, but envied them just the same. Only later, much later, did she realise that some of the 'sleepers' were dead.

Three hours or so had passed since the departure of the *Hipper,* but she had ceased to have any idea of time. The float had been passing through the night for an eternity : it was impossible to visualise the light of day. It also seemed to her that a tremendous silence reigned across the world. The howl of the gale and the crash of the waters had terrified her when she had first left the *Gustloff* : but now there was only silence. Uncanny silence. She would gladly have opted for the earlier tumult. Anything but this inexplicable silence.

The swell was still high, and the tide still swift. At times the float spun like a top on the wave crests, and only the ropes with which they'd lashed themselves to their refuge prevented the castaways from being thrown into the water. Yet there was still no sound. Not even when the weather sent it racing from crest to trough with the speed of a skier—raising not snow, but blossoming spirals of spray—did the float, in the course of its wild progress, intrude upon the hush that bound this alien scene. Completely divorced from her surroundings, and even from herself, Ilse had lost all sense of terror, and subjectivity too. Hitherto crushed, she was now resigned and calm. Even the fur coat had served to contribute to her disorientation. It had lost all semblance of its nature and purpose. No longer soft and yielding, it was glacier-smooth. The hail, the sleet and the sea-water had frozen over it. She was cocooned in ice.

Not until she had taken a beating around her face did Ilse Bauer recover her hearing, and with it the will to survive. Roused from stupor by a violent plunge of the float, a seaman had found her staring into space and mumbling to herself words that made nonsense and were formless—grotesque and ugly noises coming from the throat. He spoke to her, but she obviously did not hear him. Even when he shouted he got no response. And then, an old hand of the arctic, he realised the root cause of the trouble. The poor girl's face was frozen, frozen rigid. And her mind was frozen too. It was then that he hit her. Hit her repeatedly.

Brutal? Unorthodox? Oddly the 'cure' worked. Shocked into consciousness, Ilse once more heard the roar of the gale and the clamour of the waters . . . was once more in the world where one had to fight to live.

For Sigrid Bergfeld, salvation came in a far more gentle way

'I thought you wouldn't know where to find me,' she was

babbling in the dinghy as she saw her mother walk towards her across the water. 'I thought you'd given up looking.' And her mother smiled. She no longer felt the cold, or heard the wind. She had ceased even to fear, because all was going to be well. Her mother had found her. A deep contentment, a rosy sense of well-being embraced her like a warm blanket. Now that her mother was here, she felt snug and secure as a child.

When the body of the first of her companions to die had been slid out of the dinghy she had felt sorrow, and a certain sense of wonder. That someone should go in this way, from exposure to the weather, was outside her experience. When yet another of the little group had expired, the sense of novelty had worn off a little. Would she be the third? she had wondered.

'I thought you'd given up looking,' she found herself repeating. Her mother merely smiled, a reassuring tender smile, and suddenly there was no raft, and no shifting seascape, but a summer's sky, wide meadows and the scent of flowers.

Although the *Hipper,* and now her escort, had been forced to leave the disaster area, the naval staffs ashore still nourished hopes of a massive rescue. At the HQ of the Admiral of the Eastern Sea optimism was high. The loss of the *Gustloff* was a serious one, but would be mitigated by the way in which the Navy salvaged her survivors. The torpedo-boat *Loewe* and a sister ship of the *TZ 36* (*TZ 12*) were known to be busy among the castaways, and dispatch boats and other small craft were making their way to the scene from Gotenhafen and points west, although it would be some hours yet before they could arrive there. By first light the searchers would be reinforced by strong air patrols, and the Russian submarines would have found their position to be unstable and moved on.

But while the planning assessment was a fairly accurate one as regards the extent of the rescue effort and its timing, it failed to make allowance for the severity of the weather, and the toll it would exact among the exhausted survivors.

Bitter cold was to be expected in the Baltic in January, but the icy grip that tightened on the people of the *Gustloff* was almost unprecedently freakish in the extent of its malevolence. Between the time of the sinking and the approach of dawn there was a temperature drop of nearly ten degrees. Starting at a daunting minus-ten Centigrade—in itself a fall of ten degrees since the previous afternoon—it grew hourly colder, descending to minus-twenty. On men, women and children already badly weakened by their ordeals on the ship following the torpedoing, people completely unschooled in naval discipline and the survival procedures that went with it, the cold was an even worse enemy than the sea. Hundreds perished at its touch.

One of the wireless operators, his float having capsized, found an unlikely refuge on an ice-floe and was eventually spotted by the lookouts of a rescue ship. When they got him off, they found that his three companions—a woman and her two children, were not only dead from exposure, but had frozen solidly into the ice. 'They had become part of the floe itself,' one of the seamen later put it.

Although the *TZ 36* had lifted over five hundred survivors they had suffered so much from their experiences that scores of them died after rescue. Many more were frostbite casualties, and several of those lost their limbs. Both afloat, and later ashore, the doctors were kept busy with amputations. But even among those fortunate enough to emerge physically little the worse from the sinking and its aftermath, the weather's cruelty left mental scars that nothing could ever erase.

Eva Luck was one such : so much a victim of exposure that her clothes had frozen to her body and had to be cut from her. Only when they had nursed her back to health did they tell her that her mother and sister were lost. She was so distraught that she could say nothing by way of reply, except repeat their names, over and over again. A woman in her thirties, snatched back from the dead, had to be restrained from suicide when she heard that she was the sole survivor of what had been a happy family. Her husband had been killed at the front, and now she had lost her children. All four of them had perished following the *Gustloff*'s passing. A soldier owed his life to a particularly grisly circumstance, being sheltered by the corpses of two of his comrades. When the cold had killed them they had fallen on top of him, and thus part-shielded him from the frozen spray. At first the boarding party thought he too was dead. When it was realised that there was still life in him, they had to chisel away the ice that bound him in the frozen embrace of the dead.

Against cold of such intensity the most comprehensive plans for rescue drawn up by the men at Base were doomed to failure. 'Only thirteen miles from Hela,' they'd said at first, radiating confidence in the prospects of a massive lift of survivors. *Only* thirteen miles? For all the difference it made to the fate of the *Gustloff*'s castaways it could have been thirteen hundred. And the same held true for the men of the rescue craft. Knowing that literally every minute would bring fresh 'executions', and diminish still further the dwindling numbers of those they had come to save, they were bitter, frustrated and angry at their lot. The heavy swell, the poor visibility, and, above all, the swift lethal action of the cold ... these circumstances had conspired together to negate their effort, determined though they were, and had made them derisory. The sense of failure was acute.

The *Goettingen*, having arrived on the scene of the sinking when the submarine threat was at its most grave, had exposed herself and her passengers a score of times to the enemy's torpedoes before resuming, under orders, her interrupted voyage. Using lights and flares she had searched the area for over two hours, and had risked repeatedly sharing the *Gustloff*'s fate, yet what she had achieved by her self-sacrificial effort was almost negligible when measured against the massive toll of the disaster. Of the *Gustloff*'s six thousand plus, the *Goettingen* managed to save only twenty-two.

*'Auf einem Seemannsgrab da blühen keine Rosen,*
*Auf einem Seemannsgrab da blüht kein Blumelein.'*
*(Upon a seaman's grave no roses blossom,*
*Upon a seaman's grave no little flowers bloom.)*

As a landlubber from the east, Ilse Bauer was not familiar
with the words of the sentimental ballad that, so much beloved
by the German Navy, had been frowned on by the Party in
recent months as 'having no positive value', and even smacking
of 'defeatism'. Yet even she, however much untutored, could
see a contradiction in the remorseless, and by now so familiar,
touch of the freezing sea, hurling ice splinters onto the occupants of the float, and the flowers—yes, flowers!—that were
now travelling down from its crest. As one of them came alongside, she reached for it, and grasped at it, to see, to her stupefaction, a full-blown rose. But when, half-delirious, she raised it
to her numbed nose to scent its fragrance she could have cried
out with mortification and sense of loss. The thing dissolving
in her icy hand was no real flower, but ersatz, made of paper.
A 'flower' that probably had come from a *Gustloff* state-room :
a flower as doomed as had been the ship itself, yet she had
looked to it as a sign, an omen of hope. She decided to protest
about it all, and started to shake the man who sat beside her.
She wanted to tell him how cheated they had been. But he did
not answer. She shook him again by his strangely rigid shoulders, and he fell straight forward, to lie with his face pressed
into the ice in the bottom of the float.

It was then her turn to pass out : though not into complete
unconsciousness, but a broken sleep of nightmares. . . .


When the lookouts of the torpedo-recovery vessel *TF 19* first
sighted the dinghy it was difficult to distinguish it from an ice-

floe, so brightly did its frozen surface glitter in the dawn's pale light. Even when *TF 19* went alongside and had a closer look it seemed untenanted, and it was not until a seaman boarded it that they found the girl.

She was lying in the well of the dinghy and at first the A.B. concluded she was dead. She was as stiff as marble, and seemingly much colder. When he touched her pulse there was no reaction—no reaction that he could feel, and he was scared lest he break her wrist, it felt so brittle. Yes, the cold must have killed her, he reflected. Killed her as it had killed so many others. All the same, he couldn't be sure. Elderly by contrast with the youngsters who formed the bulk of the Kriegsmarine, he looked at her with pity. A family man, he could imagine how much this daughter must mean to those at home. No, he could not be *sure* that she was dead, despite appearances. He would bring her back with him : let *them* find out on the launch.

It wasn't an easy transfer. His feet kept sliding on the ice that encrusted every inch of the boat, and the dinghy was continually bucking—jumping up and down on the swell like a horse in a rodeo.

'Take it steady!' they yelled at him from the *TF 19*. But he needed no telling. The slightest of false steps would drop him into the drink. Worse, it would cause the girl to drop there too. And *if* there was still within her—contrary to appearances— even the faintest vestige of life, then certainly the fall would abruptly snuff it. He glanced at the *TF 19*, riding dizzily on a wavetop, and then, as it slid to the base, he pressed the unconscious girl to his chest, and jumped.

It took them several hours to bring the 'dead' Sigrid Bergfeld back to life. And several hours more to fetch her back to full awareness. All that time, the tough AB was allowed to sit beside her bunk and hold her hand. . . .


While the *TZ 36* was carrying her salvaged 'passengers' to the little port of Sassnitz, to the west of Danzig Bay, the torpedo-boat *Loewe* was tallying up her own list of survivors. They totalled 272. Including Sigrid, the *TF 19* had picked up seven more. For such hard work and skilful seamanship the haul seemed meagre.

It was left to the inconspicuous *VP 1703* to perform the final act in the rescue saga, and add to the total saved one small, but precious, life.

## CHAPTER FOURTEEN

## *The Tide Rolls On*

IT WAS seven hours after the *Gustloff*'s descent to death, when into the disaster area, by then completely deserted, came a single-funnelled, rusty, and generally seedy-looking little patrol boat, straining her overworked engines as she battled against the sea. The rescue fleet proper had long since left for home, and as *1703*, maid of all work without a name, made her belated appearance on the scene, those aboard her had little hope of doing anything particularly useful, and no hope at all of encountering survivors.

'It's inconceivable,' said the Reserve Lieutenant commanding, 'that anyone is still alive. All that's left us is the dirty job of picking up the dead.'

As he spoke, the thermometer had dropped to minus-20 Centigrade, and the Verpostenboot was making cautious progress between a score or more of drifting ice-floes. Against the wan first light, gusts of near gale force were throwing fresh flurries of snow.

'Ship's company of a floating morgue. That's *our* bloody luck,' declaimed a plaintive voice from the lookout post, but no one laughed. Not even an extra ration of Schnapps could lift their gloom or act as buffer against the morbidity of their mission, accentuated as it was by the diabolical behaviour of the weather. 'Inconceivable' indeed that any of the *Gustloff*'s people could still be living in this merciless refrigerator. Familiar though they were with the harshness of the Baltic in winter, the men had never known it to be as bad as this, and freely said so.

As he squinted into the greyness that marked the division of the waters from the dark, Petty Officer Werner Fisch felt the cold stab through his oilskins and get under the heavy monkey jacket that he wore beneath them. Its knife-point played excruciatingly on his bones and his feet were numb. A sod of a night, he summarised. At the best of times no one in his right mind would have chosen the ancient *VP 1703* as ideal for a jaunt in the January Baltic. But this was the worst of times, and for Fisch the going was particularly tough. It wasn't as though he was an enthusiastic youngster, bursting with health and vigour. In his mid-forties the P.O. was no fanatic. He was conscientious in his duties, but hunted no medals, and the Party's impassioned rabble-rousing left him completely unmoved. He had a wife ashore, living in Rostock-Gehlsdorf, and he valued the home comforts, though never more so than now. A sod of a night, and the dawn looked like being no better!

It was just after 4 a.m. when the Lieutenant ordered the searchlight to be switched on, but even this did little to pierce the murk, let alone give any clue as to the extent of the toll exacted by the tragedy. Fractured timbers, a scrap or two of clothing drifted out of the murk of snow and sleet, nudged gently the boat's sides, and then disappeared again. Once, Fisch sighted a ship's oar and two empty lifebelts too, but otherwise, for all the evidence she had left of her sudden passing, the *Wilhelm Gustloff* might never have existed.

They had been searching for an hour before the lookout hailed: 'Object ahead!' Through smarting eyes and lashes turned hard and brittle, they saw to starboard a shadowy outline. Reappearing, vanishing and then rolling back into view, it was only slightly whiter than the foam of the breaking wavecaps. 'A lifeboat,' Fisch excitedly exclaimed.

Seconds later, the lookout shouted: 'There are two people aboard her.'

Impossible that anyone from the *Gustloff* could still be alive.
Fisch knew it, even as a quick look through the night-glasses
confirmed the accuracy of the sighting. Chilled as he was, the
P.O.'s hands were trembling, and it took him some time to
focus. Two people were in the boat, and there might be more.
But they gave not the slightest sign of life, let alone feeling. Not
even the faintest flutter of a hand answered the yells of the
would-be rescuers.

'Stiffs?' queried someone.

Fisch gave an impatient shrug.

It was probably less than minutes, but it seemed a hundred
times longer, before the *1703* managed to get close to the boat,
and still there was no reaction from the silent 'crew'. They rode
up and down with the boat as if built into it. They were so rigid
that they could have been monuments, carved from ice.

'They've tied themselves fast,' the Lieutenant said. 'So as not
to be washed overboard.'

Fisch, briefly fidgeting with the tapes of his lifejacket, hardly
heard him. He was far too preoccupied with thoughts of the
job ahead. With another man, he was waiting the order to
board.

'When I shout *go*,' the Lieutenant said. 'It'll be then or never.
No time for hanging about. . . .'

Boarding a dinghy in this swinish weather was no joke. Nice
calculation and timing would be required. Fervently Fisch
hoped that they would get it. The patrol boat was rolling
heavily, and needed careful handling in order to get alongside.
On the one hand was the danger of her ramming her quarry.
On the other the necessity of getting her close enough for a
jump. No one fancied a swim in this merciless sea.

'*Go!*' the Lieutenant yelled.

They went. . . .

Fisch almost fell into the boat, his sea-boots stubbing into a heap of unexpected obstacles in its well. Clothing of all sorts . . . coats, dresses, underwear even . . . he stared at this mixed cargo almost in disbelief.

'Must have been lifted by a rescue ship,' his mate exlaimed. 'Those that were still alive. . . .'

Fisch gingerly approached the nearest of the silent figures, to find it was a woman. She was slumped forward over the seat to which she had been roped. There was no reaction to his touch. Her body was as unyielding as cold iron. He caught a brief impression of the once attractive face—a purple-grey mask from which stared sightless eyes. A stiff, all right! He turned to his companion. 'What about *yours*?'

'He's had it, too,' came the answer.

But the motionless pair were not the boat's only occupants. Lying between the thwarts were two more bodies, and, at the sight of them, Fisch found himself wanting to spew. A boy of about ten, and a girl in her early teens. They too had fallen victims of the cold.

'What's happening?' bawled the Lieutenant through the megaphone.

Fisch gave the sign that meant a scrub-out. 'Both of them kaput,' he answered. 'And two kids dead as well. . . .'

'Okay then, you'd better come back. . . .'

The Lieutenant's voice was edged with a certain impatience. He was in a hurry to get the boat under way again, and proceed with the rest of his mission. There would doubtless be other dinghies, and floats as well, to explore. There was no time to waste in fretting for the few among so many.

'Just give me a moment, Herr Leutnant!'

Fisch was too old a hand to allow himself to be rushed, not when there were benefits to be achieved by dawdling. And now, recovering from his initial nausea, he turned to the task of doing a little salvage. Amongst the pile of clothing at his feet were items that could possibly come in useful. What the dead couldn't wear, the living might be grateful for : if of course there were

still any of the *Gustloff*'s people living. It was then, as he
rummaged in the well, that he found the baby. . . .

Only later, after he had returned to the patrol boat and they
were trying to revive the child in the fuggy apology for a cabin
that served as Captain's quarters, did Fisch have time to spare
a thought for the mystery of it all, and ponder on the devotion
that had enabled the little one to survive the carnage that had
followed the sinking. The child—a boy—was no more than
fifteen months old, yet the tragedy that had claimed so many
of the strong had passed it by. Fisch found himself speculating
on how this had come about.

Perhaps the boy's mother had been the woman in the boat.
So was the man the father? Or had they both been strangers
to each other, and to the baby too? Maybe the boy's parents
had not been able to leave the ship, but had found a place in
the lifeboat for their son that was denied to them? And the
other two children—could they have been related? Suddenly
Fisch shook off these speculations as being profitless. The child
had been orphaned—he was convinced of that, and the whys
and wherefores did not really matter.

In spite of the thickness of the blankets, sufficient of the cold
had penetrated to force them to cut them from the baby. They
were impossible to shift, except by using the knife. They were
as stiff as boards.

'Poor little bugger,' the Lieutenant exclaimed. 'God knows
what sort of future he can expect.'

It was then as they thawed out his charge and, using a
tablespoon, gently plied him with ersatz milk, that Fisch came
to a sudden but irrevocable decision : one that was to change
the whole pattern of his life, and that of his wife as well. To
complete their married happiness only one thing had been lacking, and here, surely, was a sign that Providence had provided
it. Both Fisch and his wife had yearned desperately for a
child, and now had come this strange deliverance from the
deep.

'God knows what sort of future he can expect,' the Lieutenant had said.

If the boy was not claimed, he would be brought up as Fisch's son !

Ilse Bauer was screaming when she eventually awoke. Screaming with terror. The memory of her ordeal in the barn, oddly interwoven with the scenes on the *Gustloff*'s boat-deck, had made a nightmare that was almost as vivid, and as terrible, as the reality. Beating down on her was a merciless light, a ball of fire on her aching eyes, and she was vaguely aware of cowled figures behind the light. Threatening figures, they seemed to her, and with intent to murder. 'Don't kill him,' she cried. 'He has done no harm. For God's sake don't kill him.'

They were hustling her father to the back of the farmcart once again . . . these men with the fur hats and shapeless combat blouses. Once more she'd hear the sharp burst of their machine-pistols, and see her mother throw herself on the crumpled and bleeding body. 'For God's sake don't kill him,' she implored, though knowing it was useless. And then she passed out.

'Whatever is the girl babbling about this time,' queried the Surgeon-Commander. 'And who are we trying to kill ?'

'Some fantasy of the mind,' said the SBA resignedly, 'or maybe something she has remembered from the past. They've had strange things happen to them, these refugees from the east.'

'And so young, too,' sighed the Surgeon-Commander.

'She'd a bad time on the float as well, or so they say. Her clothes had iced into her when we picked her up.'

'Well, she'll soon be back on her feet again, so she's luckier than most.'

Father . . . mother . . . sister . . . brother . . . Ilse Bauer was not alone in experiencing the sadness of family bereavement. On the *Loewe* they were case-hardened to tales of tragedy far more recent in their wounding. Carrying on with the rescue operation at the point where *TZ 36* had been obliged to leave off, the torpedo-boat had managed to retrieve 220 people from the weather and the ocean, and a good half of them had lost their closest relatives in the *Gustloff*'s sinking. Ilse was fortunate in that she had emerged from the aftermath of the wreck without any permanent damage—'damage' in the sense of physical injury. On the *Loewe* they were not psychiatrists, and could not answer for the mind.

'What a mess!' reflected the Surgeon-Commander. 'What a bloody mess it all is. Five thousand or more dead, a mere handful of living, and among that handful the limbless and the blind. People scarred for life.'

'Wonder what they'll make of it ashore, sir?' queried the SBA. 'Wonder what they'll make of *her*? When they can get her into a proper hospital. . . .'


'Wonder what they'll make of it ashore?' While Ilse was being nursed slowly back to health, and Fisch was still marvelling at the discovery he had made in the lifeboat, Lieutenant Fleischer, back on Gotenhafen, was grimly accepting the fact that he, so recently the proud bridegroom, was now a widower. Ruth could never have survived the *Gustloff*'s passing. He was sure of that. He had already heard too much from the returning rescuers to credit she could have stayed alive in conditions where so many thousands—tougher by far than she—had succumbed to the horrors that had accompanied the sinking.

Since the moment when it had fallen to him to read the text of the retransmitted S.O.S., Fleischer's desperate despair for his bride had reigned unabated and all the evidence now pointed to it being justified.

After they had recovered from the initial shock of the liner's torpedoing, his fellow officers aboard the *Lutzow* had been relatively optimistic in their assessment of the chances of mass-

rescue, but Fleischer had been unable to share their mood, or
respond to well-meant efforts to cheer him up. But what had
since put the seal on the Lieutenant's depression was when,
through the same cruel accident of duty that had made him one
of the first to hear of the *Gustloff*'s plight, he had intercepted
the news of the *Admiral Hipper*'s withdrawal. At this, and the
reports of the rapidly worsening weather, even the super-opti-
mists had begun to lose heart, and Fleischer had felt his misery
envelop him like the tide. Ruth was dead. He was sure of it.

Survivors were still being picked up but it was obvious that
they would not amount to very many : not when compared with
the masses originally embarked. The *Loewe* would have space
for only a fragment of the total in need of help, and the other
craft involved could not cope with many more. With few illusions about the degree of hardship those escaping from the
*Gustloff* must have experienced before the work of rescue had
got under way, Fleischer felt it was far too much to hope that
Ruth could have been among the lucky few. So inexperienced
in the requirements of survival . . . so unlikely to have been
able to resist the stampede of thousands . . . she would probably never have succeeded even in leaving the ship. In fact, at
one stage, his pessimism was so acute that while searching for
news of her he almost dreaded hearing it, for fear of what that
news would be. Too old a hand to think that death at sea was
something that struck painlessly and swiftly, he dreaded hearing of the manner of her passing. Say that the end had come
for her in torture and terror?

It was only by a tremendous effort of will that Fleischer eventually steeled himself to face the fact that he could not continue
to nurse his grief in secret, but had a responsibility to the living
as well as to the dead. Someone would have to warn Ruth's
parents of their daughter's probable fate—break the news gently
before they reeled to the shock of the official announcement.
Someone must try to soften the pain that *they* would feel, and
that 'someone' could only be him !

Although the much-invoked 'requirements of State Security' still imposed a press and radio blackout on the loss of the *Gustloff*, word of it got around with unprecedented speed. This was partly due to the fact that the Navy's rescue operation had been launched from such a broad base. With the ships involved in it being drawn from widely separate areas, from Pomerania to Kiel, thousands were soon abuzz with fact and speculation. But not all sources of this monumental leak were strictly naval in their origins. Many civilian elements had also been in the know. The onset of the Russian land offensive had alarmed millions of westerners with relatives and friends in the threatened territories and latterly considerable efforts had been made to reassure them of their safety. Thus for days before the sailing of the *Gustloff* and her sister transports, inspired rumours of evacuation had been plentiful, even though, in quaint contrast, the official dialogue of the regime had been one of Wagnerian defiance.

Again, the very magnitude of the evacuation, in terms of numbers, had necessarily required the provision of reception facilities of proportionate size and scope. Party organisations and helpers had to be alerted. The job could not be left to the military alone, and inevitably these had had to cope with a legion of requests for information. Fleischer was merely one among the many who were suffering agonies of uncertainty concerning the fate of loved ones; and for most the reality was to prove more cruel than even the worst of their apprehensions.

Eva Luck's father clutched her tightly to him when the two were reunited in the West. His wife and his eldest daughter had perished in the disaster. Eva was all that he had left. . . . For another man, in action against the British in Holland, there was tragedy that was probably even more hard to bear. Although long since remarried, and with his second family now well into their teens, he will never forget the brutal impact of the blow that fell on him in the first week of February, nine days after the sinking. He had lost not only his wife and three small children in the *Gustloff*, but also his parents and his sister-in-law. The entire family had been living together ever since he had been posted to the west, and had owed their embarkation in the liner to 'influence' that he himself had managed to procure!

Only here and there among the multitude whose lives were linked with the liner's fate (directly and indirectly they were estimated to total 30,000) was initial grief transformed by later news into relief and joy. Transferred by a rescue craft on to a former liner that had been hurriedly transformed into an accommodation ship for the *Gustloff*'s survivors, a woman was reunited with her four young children, from whom she had been separated during the rush for the boats—children she had given up for dead! An elderly man who had been picked up from the water, and returned to consciousness ashore, was almost inconsolable over the 'loss' of his wife—only to find she had preceded him in the *TZ 36* and was being nursed back to health in the same hospital as himself. And there was also the lucky chance that saved a young teenage girl—snatched from death when the light of a flare caught the glitter of the ice that formed a skull-cap on her hair. But such happy exceptions to the general rule were rare indeed, and passed almost unnoticed as the full extent of the catastrophe began to become apparent to the folk ashore.

The day after the *Gustloff*'s sinking, Grand Admiral Doenitz, in conference with the Fuehrer, took a philosophic view of the ship's painful fate. In the minutes of the meeting it is recorded that: 'In connection with the sinking of the passenger liner *Wilhelm Gustloff* by submarine torpedoes on the outer route of the Stolpe Bank, the C-in-C Navy declares that with the extensive transports in the Baltic Sea, it was realised from the start that there would be losses. Painful as any loss may be, it is very fortunate that more have not occurred. . . .'

People on stretchers, groaning at each clumsy step of their

bearers down the gangplank from the rescue craft to the
jetty . . . stokers blanketed to conceal the flesh that had been
peeled from them by the steam . . . bloated corpses, at which
the fish had nibbled . . . these indeed bore testimony to just
how 'painful' had been the *Gustloff's* quittance.

The lone sortie launched by the *VP 1703* was the last of its
kind, and marked the end of the attempt to rescue anything
living from the disaster. At HQ they knew that no purpose
could be served by further effort—not in this refrigerator of a
sea and besides the ships were now needed for matters of more
importance to the Reich. Gotenhafen, which only three days
before had seemed so close to collapse, was now fighting back,
and fighting back with a force and energy that had taken everyone by surprise. 'You will yield not an inch,' the Fuehrer had
commanded, and the last of the Wehrmacht's resources had
been hurled into the battle. The Navy, too, was involved in
the process of counter-attack, and was deploying for that purpose every weapon it possessed. Those ex-'*Gustloffs*' who had
been moved from the ship before her departure had been drafted
into the line to serve as soldiers, while behind them the warships opened a fierce bombardment of the Russian armour,
holding it in check, and then forcing it to fall back.

It was not until April that the disputed base finally surrender-
ed, and even then the Kriegsmarine managed to play a decisive
role, snatching thousands of soldiers from beneath the Russian
noses, and removing them to more congenial captivity in the
West. Nor was the effort of the surface fleet confined entirely
to Danzig Bay and its immediate surroundings. The ships which
had supported to the last the garrison of Memel, evacuating the
major part of it, then covered the army's withdrawal from the
Courland, even further to the North.

For the *Lutzow,* and for Lieutenant Fleischer, these were
busy days indeed, but the latter was no longer in despair and
grief. Although Germany was crumbling all around him, he
knew that he had still very much to live for. Ruth had been

back home with her parents when they'd received his telegram —the telegram that had given the news of her own death!

Immediately, she had written back to him, but not for a month did her letter catch up with the overworked ship, and by then he had long since known that his fears had proved unfounded and his nightmare was over. Before the last direct communication links were severed between what was to become the 'two Germanies'—West and East—the newly-weds had managed to speak to each other on the telephone, and Fleischer had returned to war a happier man.

It was on April 9th that the *Lutzow* went to her death, only to be marvellously resurrected. Victim of a concentrated R.A.F. attack at Swinemunde, she was hit repeatedly, lost forty casualties and was sunk. But the ship had gone down in shallow water and, with timber patches secured across the gaping holes that the bombs had left, she was raised within days and promptly set to service as a sort of floating fortress, her big guns blazing defiance at the Russians. Only when her last round had been expended was the *Lutzow* finally destroyed: blown to pieces by explosive charges detonated by her crew.

For *Hipper* ('the Lucky Ship') was reserved a different fate. Having safely delivered her wounded passengers to western ports, she, like the *Lutzow*, experienced the unwelcome attentions of the R.A.F. Heavily bombed while in dry dock at Kiel, she was knocked out of the war for good, and was later taken over by the British.

For the *TZ 36* the end came in April, less than five months from the date of her first commissioning and only nine weeks after her devoted work of rescue among the *Gustloff* survivors. After her success in so narrowly evading the Russian torpedoes in January, it was her bad fortune to encounter a Russian mine.

But what of the lesser personalities—the human beings? The men, women and children whose fortunes had once been so closely interwoven with the comings and goings of these ships and their enemies, and had formed with them a part, however minute, of the tapestry of battle? What future was there for the living who had been snatched from the midst of the dead?

For Sigrid Bergfeld, as for Frau Fleischer too, the horror of her experience on the *Gustloff* was followed by convalescence, recovery and normality. Eva Luck, eventually recovering from her grief, worked for a while as a secretary during the immediate aftermath of Germany's defeat, and then embarked on a stage career. But even the most far-fetched theme developed for the theatre could never rival, let alone surpass the fantastic ordeal she had experienced when adrift in the icy Baltic.

Perhaps curiously, Ilse Bauer emerged from the disaster in considerably better health than she had experienced in the months before it. It was as though the horrors of the sinking had served to part-obliterate from her mind the memory of those previous horrors to which she had been subjected by the Russian patrol, and, after hospital treatment, she began to live a normal life again. Today, she is a married woman with a family, though her husband has no idea of the circumstances that drove her to the *Gustloff*'s treacherous refuge.

A month or so after the *Wilhelm Gustloff*'s destruction, and just prior to the other two great 'drownings' as they became known—the sinking of the transports *General Steuben* and *Goya*—Adolf Hitler, commenting on the 'low percentage' of shipping losses during the evacuation of the eastern ports, made one of his rare puns: 'Better ten percent sunk,' he quipped, 'than ninety percent Siberia.'

Rapturously received by his entourage, the remark, though seemingly logical, might have struck the near-relatives of the *Gustloff*'s lost as being somewhat lacking in taste.

## ... *Who Didn't Drown.*

THE FLOAT came in with the tide, bounced gently on the beach, recoiled in company with the receding wave and then came again, this time to lodge itself on the snow-crusted sand.

Down from the dunes of Hela came three soldiers at the run, to grab the rim of the float with mittened hands to prevent it escaping once more, while they inspected the body that lay spreadeagled in its centre.

The man was in the bottle-green of an officer of the Waffen SS and in his frozen brow was a neat round hole. The runes on his right collar patch were splashed with scarlet.

Gingerly one of the soldiers tried to ease the Walther from his hand, but the pistol was gripped too tightly, and the hand was so brittle, that he did not persevere. 'His bones will crack in two if I try too hard,' he mumbled.

As they started to ease the officer's body from the float they found that his cap had been lying beneath his stomach.

Only very lightly flecked with ice, the death's head on the cap band winked in the winter sun.

One of the Damned hadn't drowned!